A. Horsley Hinton

A Handbook of Illustration

outlook

A. Horsley Hinton

A Handbook of Illustration

1st Edition | ISBN: 978-3-75239-225-8

Place of Publication: Frankfurt am Main, Germany

Year of Publication: 2020

Outlook Verlag GmbH, Germany.

A HANDBOOK OF ILLUSTRATION

BY

A. HORSLEY HINTON

CHAPTER I.

Introduced to this country, in round numbers, some fifty years ago, Photography has progressed beyond its contemporaries of the present century. It has obtained a hold upon the people, entering equally into their work and their amusements; the speed, the reality, the brilliancy of it fit it peculiarly for the age into which it has been born. It has survived, and will survive, amidst the decay of other things, because of its extraordinary adaptability to changing circumstances, its readiness to meet altering tastes and requirements; versatile in aspect, elastic in its application.

Amidst all its adaptations of modern date, in none has it been more successful than in that to which this book is devoted: that wherein photography, directly or indirectly, is employed to introduce into our literature expressions of thought, which are better so conveyed than by written or printed words. Be the language never so rich in words, or the writer's power in using them never so great, a clearer and a more lasting impression may be conveyed, even to the cultivated, and certainly to the popular mind, by the arrangement of lines and markings in such form as may be felt to actually represent the objects, and indicate the relative position and size of other objects or parts of the same.

This may be said to be the primary and normal function of an Illustration. Throughout the pages of this book, and to whatever extent the student may practise the methods herein described, it may be well to keep very clearly in mind the legitimate function of an illustration, namely: to describe, to portray, and to do this *chiefly* as an auxiliary to written language.

To such a kind belongs the rude scratchings of the primæval man, whose limited powers of speech forbade his adequately describing the forms of those creatures whose pursuit meant life, whose disregard would mean death, and of such kind were the hieroglyphics of the East. Nay, who shall say that the very forms of letters themselves are not the outcome of early effort to convey to the eye of another what might otherwise only have been imperfectly communicated through other senses: a means to an end; a servant, a tool, in the hands of him who would wield it.

But in the beginning there was a making of drawings and designs which had another purpose. The gourd, or rough clay vessel, was graved and marked with devices and forms suggested by the curves and shapes in Nature, but this was merely for decoration; to please the eye, and not to serve any purpose but to give pleasure. A means to an end in this sense perhaps, but note that the end was in the commencement of it, and went no further after completion; it gave pleasure to the beholder and no more, and nothing more was intended or asked. Thus was Art born—not to teach, nor to explain, nor to illustrate.

AN ESSEX LANDSCAPE.

Half-tone from oil sketch in monochrome. (Original 10⅛ x 6½*).* [See

p. 51.]

Nor is this distinction out of place in the present work. The tendency to-day is too often to make a pretty picture rather than a good illustration; to sacrifice accuracy to beauty; to strive rather after the æsthetic pleasure in art, than the truth and fidelity of illustration. The artist is what he is from the possession of certain instinctive attributes which he is powerless to teach to another, whereas the simpler and expressive forms of draughtsmanship *may be attained by almost all*. From confusing art with illustration we find a man saying "I cannot do this, or that, because I am no artist," and it is with a hope of placing in the hands of such, at least to some extent, a means of graphic expression, that the present book has been undertaken.

Take also such a simple matter as a letter from a friend, and notice how often words alone fail to convey a correct impression, yet a few lines of simple form at once present a graphic description.

3

Mr. Blackburn gives a capital example of such a case in his "Art of Illustration." He says: "A newspaper correspondent is in a boat on one of the Italian lakes, and wishes to describe the scene on a calm summer day. This is how he proceeds:

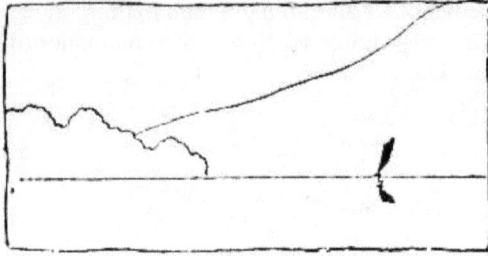

"'We are shut in by mountains,' he says, 'but the blue lake seems as wide as the sea. On a rocky promontory on the left hand the trees grow down to the water's edge and the banks are precipitous, indicating the great depth of this part of the lake. The water is as smooth as glass; on its surface is one vessel, a heavily laden market boat' (and so on). There is no need to repeat it all; but when half a column of word-painting had been written (and well written) the correspondent failed to present the picture clearly to the eye without these *four* explanatory lines (no more) which should of course have been sent with his letter."

In the same way small sketch plans (no matter how roughly made) are of great assistance in describing the position of a fire, a murder, or anything else of public importance; not to mention the value such descriptive lines often are in private letters.

Whilst, then, Art and Illustration are distinct, and much of the latter may be within the reach of many to whom the former is impossible, there is no reason why either should needlessly offend the canons of the other. Art—seeking, as it should, to awaken a sense of pleasure in the beautiful—adheres to truth, in idea if not in fact. Illustration, which portrays fact truthfully, may yet do so in such manner as shall not annoy the cultivated and artistic senses; and this is the art of illustration.

Here, as in other matters, much depends on a knowledge and exercise of the mere technique or craftsmanship: the means to be employed, and the manner of employing them.

With pen or pencil we might satisfactorily produce such a diagram or drawing as should *illustrate* our speech, but the exigencies of such gigantic institutions of civilisation as books, magazines, and newspapers, demand that the same illustration shall be presented to thousands of readers at the same time. In former times the original drawing was copied by craftsmen on to wood or metal, and then carved so that a "block," containing the design in relief, might be set up in the printing press and printed in conjunction with the letterpress type.

Wonderful skill did the wood-engraver acquire in reproducing the original and in interpreting the artist's idea; but his work took time, which had to be paid for, and sometimes the artist found that in passing through the intermediary wood-engraver, his intention had been wrongly construed, and even a departure made from the accuracy of his drawing. Then came Photography, and it was found possible to photograph the original on to the surface of the block instead of drawing it. It was next found possible, under given conditions, to substitute for the engraver a purely mechanical means, whereby the surface of the block was suitably carved to print with ink the requisite design.

Thus a photographic and chemical *process* supplants the hand-work of the engraver, and a perfect replica of the original, in no way dependent upon the personal ability of the engraver, is obtained. The same process, working blindly, produces a facsimile equivalent to the artist's own drawing; and does so with such speed, and at such small expense, that for one penny we may purchase to-day a newspaper filled with exact copies of drawings of events which happened only yesterday. Thousands of books and papers, the world over, are now replete with illustrations: the expense of producing which by the older methods would have made impossible such welcome additions to the printed page.

Nor does it appear that the gigantic dimensions, and high state of perfection, which Process illustration has reached, in any way represents the limit of its possibilities in either respect. It has been reasonably conjectured that in the near future every newspaper and periodical publication will be illustrated, and almost each day sees some advancement, some improvement, in the daily practice of the various processes of reproduction, so that in writing a book of the present kind it is difficult to keep the information therein contained fully abreast of the times. While it is in the hands of the printer some new thing may be found out, some new application of a method successfully attempted, which shall make the novelty of yesterday give place to the invention of to-day.

The pride of the *littérateur* may make him feel that the use of pictures, as an assistance to writing, indicates incapacity or feebleness on the part of the author. Yet, able as is the description of such familiar characters as Mr. Pecksniff, Pickwick, Jingle, and others, how various would have been the idea conjured up by different readers, were it not for the inimitable drawings of Cruickshank or "Phiz." Were not Shakespeare's characters intended to be illustrated—not by drawings perhaps, but by "living pictures"?

And, finally, out of the simple instruments for illustration there has been evolved a greater thing. The same means as are employed to reproduce the draughtsman's drawing, may also reproduce, and place in the hands of the multitude, reproductions of the works of great master artists; so that something of the treasures of the Pitti, and the Louvre, may be seen in English homes to-day. The same simple methods, used for mere illustration, have been wrestled with by those who possess art as a birthright from the gods, and through their efforts our books may now contain pictures (process reproductions) which are full of fine artistic feeling; not merely illustrating the text, but awakening a sense of pleasure and exaltation at the representation of nature's beauties. Decorative pages, ornate with noble designs, brighten a book like gleaming crystals in a rich but dark mine, and relieve the monotony of too perfect a symmetry. A chapter heading, a tail piece, a decorated initial, and here and there a picture page, exert an influence like sparkling spring and smiling flowers, for joy and sweet refreshment by the way.

CHAPTER II.

A NEGLECTED FIELD.

A form of book illustration too much neglected, and one possessing peculiar advantages, is Margina Illustration. Decorated or illustrated margins may be associated in idea with the early monastic work, when the solitude and gloom of the recluse's life was relieved by the little enjoyment which must have attended the illumination of holy books, but it is not quite the purely decorative to which I would refer.

In some modern editions, in which an old style is affected, a wide margin on the top, bottom, and outer edge of the letterpress is preserved so wide that ample space might be found to introduce such trifling illustrations as would be amply sufficient to fix an impression or suggest to the imagination of the reader ideas which the mere letterpress might fail to awaken.

LINE REPRODUCTION FROM PEN SKETCH.

(Original 13 x 9 inches.)

Too often our illustrations in books are separated from the text to such a degree that a continuity of idea is all but impossible. We read, perhaps —"Night wanes—the vapours round the mountains curl'd melt into morn, and Light awakes the world. Man has another day to swell the past," &c., &c., &c.; but long before we come to the page which illustrates this delightfully pictorial passage from one of Lord Byron's romantic works we read—"'Tis morn—'tis noon—assembled in the hall. The gathered chieftains come to Otho's call:" and not perhaps until we have passed the third or fourth stanza, and are trying to picture in our minds the brilliant assemblage of Spanish chieftains, and the fierce challenge of the accused Lara terminating with "Demand thy life!" do we turn over a page and confront a dainty illustration of the opening lines "Night wanes," &c.—an interruption as undesirable and distracting as when the lecturer, through some mistake in the arranging of his lantern slides, sees projected on the screen a photogram of the grim walls of Newgate Prison, when, with the words "I will now show you a picture of where some of England's heroes have found a resting-place," he expected his assistant to put up a slide of Westminster Abbey. It is not always possible even to get our book illustrations to face the matter which refers to it, and even if that can be arranged, or the illustration can actually come into the same page, the act of turning from text to picture means an interruption and severing the continuous thought. Could our illustrations appear in the margin, between the lines, mingled with the letterpress, how smoothly we might *read* the *illustrations* along with the text, and how bright and pleasing would the pages appear!

I have given a specimen page which may serve to better show the idea.

We will suppose some book of travel or poetry be set up in type by the printer, and a proof copy be made up with broad margins under the direction of the illustrator, who then takes it in hand and decorates each page as desired; or the pages are pulled as proofs on two or three kinds of paper, smooth for pen work, rough for crayon, or medium for wash drawings—what delightful variety might be secured! When the artist has added his marginal and inter-paragraph illustrations the pages are photo-reproduced, the complete block including both letterpress and drawings.

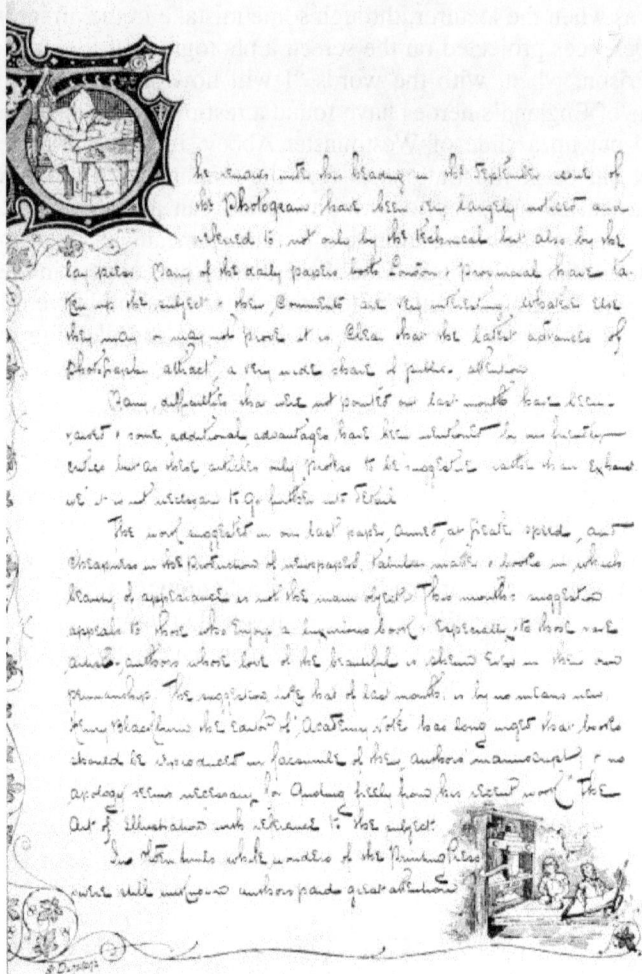

PENNED BY W.T. WHITEHEAD.

(Original 15 x 12 inches.)

Of course the illustrations, if confined to the margins, could be reproduced separately, and set up with the type in the same form. In the example I have given on page 15, the letterpress was set up by the printer to occupy a given space, the type used being a clear, bold letter. This was printed from on two or three kinds of paper, and handed to me to add the illustrative matter. The proof used was about thirteen by nine inches, and this was subsequently reproduced by a simple zinco process to the size here shown.

Of course the amount of letterpress possible on each page is small if the illustrating be carried to any great extent. An edition of Shakespeare's works treated in this fashion would of itself constitute a small library, but for smaller works, or for single plays or single poems, many a plain piece of reading might be by such means converted into a very delightful and beloved book.

I have often thought that in fiction, when we read that the dainty little *billet doux* slipped under the door, written in my lady's delicate and graceful style; or, the mysterious letter handed to the hero written in a strange handwriting "ran as follows," how much more forcible the thing would be if the author had given us a facsimile of the letter. I never read a letter in a story without feeling it was the author of the romance, instead of the character in the book, who composed the letter. Thus an author might, in addition to feature, figure, and dress, give us a fine suggestion of his *dramatis personæ* by showing a little bit of their handwriting.

CHAPTER III.

THE THEORY AND PRINCIPLES OF ILLUSTRATION.

Here it will probably be well to consider the different classes into which illustrations naturally seem to fall, and this because it is the common custom to regard the contents of an illustrated book as all belonging to one.

Perhaps the simplest and most spontaneous form of illustration is seen when one is describing a position or locality, and takes pencil and paper to draw a rough plan showing this or that road, cross-road, turning, &c. We do this without any forethought, without any artistic ability, and never for a moment considering that we are fulfilling the first theoretical function of the illustrator, and we make this sketch-plan partly because we could not so graphically describe what we wish in words; and, again, the drawing will produce a more lasting impression upon the person appealed to, and that without so great an effort of memory on his part. "Seeing is believing," and to *see* is also to *remember*. It is the same with the diagrams which illustrate the problems of Euclid, a tourist's map, an architect's plan; these are all illustrations of a diagrammatic kind.

Only a little higher in the scale are the illustrations in scientific and physiological books. I say *higher*, because of the difficulties attaching to the photographing of such objects, and their more complex forms, which sometimes necessitate their being drawn from the objects at first hand by one possessing some amount of skill as a draughtsman. But the intention is to explain the text, added to which is perhaps the special office of enabling the student to recognise and identify the particular animal or vegetable structure, or a certain rock formation or crystal, when found; for which purpose it is of primary importance that the essential and specific characters of the particular object are carefully portrayed, and the entire figure be of faultless accuracy.

This same quality must also be secured in topographical views with which the book of travels, with its description of far-distant places and people, is illustrated; it is in this class of drawings that there is most danger of a desire to make a pretty picture—overwhelming the purely descriptive or explanatory function.

The representation of the principal characters in a story, with which it is the custom to illustrate a novel or work of fiction, has often appeared to me to be one of the least successful departments of illustration. Probably this arises from the fact that the artist has no actual models to work from; he creates, out of the author's description, imaginary beings, and portrays them accordingly. Therefore, unless author and artist have been in very close communication, it is as likely as not that the artist may get a conception of certain characters quite remote from the author's intention. At least, it must have occurred to many a reader to find the pictures in a favourite novel often quite fail to realise the ideal which he had himself formed of the hero or heroine, of whom, at the very outset, he had conjured up an image and an environment.

Somewhat lately the experiment has been made of illustrating fiction with actual photograms from life, in which case the illustrator must select with great care individuals answering very exactly to the descriptions given, and use these as models grouped as required.

Obviously this method must be confined to such books whose plot is laid in comparatively recent times and in ordinary scenes of life; for the difficulties, which are in any case great, assume insurmountable proportions when one conceives the idea of illustrating by photograms such books as "Robinson Crusoe," "Pilgrim's Progress," or "Don Quixote."

PEN DRAWING BY W.T. WHITEHEAD.
(*Original* **8 x 5.**)

The ideal condition would be for the author to illustrate his own writings, then indeed should we be sure of getting a glimpse of the character intended; and we can imagine with what care he would fashion the child of his imagination.

Failing this, the author should control to a greater extent the work of the man who is to illustrate his writings, a point far too often overlooked in the making of a book.

It will be seen that in this section of illustration the draughtsman draws upon his imagination, so that, to some extent at least, his art is *creative*. It must, however, be borne in mind that he is not at liberty to paint or draw his own unaided imaginings; he is merely interpreting another's words into a graphic representation; so that, be he never so fine an artist, his art, like Pegasus in harness, is restrained under the yoke of the illustrator.

We may, however, find illustration ascending a step higher towards the sphere of art proper and creative, and that is in the *edition de luxe*, in which, with or without printed matter, we have plates which are pictures in the best sense, and appeal chiefly, or exclusively, to the æsthetic sense. Also in some dramatic works, in poetry, and in some prose, there is a much wider scope for the imagination of the artist, and we have high-class books of a real artistic merit.

PEN DRAWING BY W.T. WHITEHEAD.

(*Original* 8 x 2.)

One other notable form of illustration remains, and that is the purely decorative. This is seen to advantage in the book-plates in which a device bears the name of the owner and is affixed to each book; to revive which custom an effort has happily been made of late. In allegorical figures and scrollwork on title-pages, at heads of chapters, in borders, in large initial letters, at the termination of a chapter, or a design interspersed with the type on a page, and in many other forms beyond the prescribed shape which its position determines, there is little to restrict the artist. Some examples of designs for book-plates were recently given in that excellent magazine *The Studio*; and some interesting and wholly praiseworthy "initials," formed on an actual photogram, appeared recently in *The Photogram*. These are two instances out of the many which may be seen on every hand, and in this connection I have long felt that photograms from nature might be more largely applied to book illustration or decoration.

Thus I have endeavoured to indicate the principal uses of illustrations. Now in every work of art, its strength and its success are dependent in a great measure upon its composition and purpose possessing simplicity and unity, and I think that it cannot be too deeply impressed upon the illustrator that singleness of purpose will be a strong contributory to success.

If the purpose of the illustration be to explain or to describe, then let it do that at the sacrifice, if need be, of all else; and if, at the same time, it be possible to introduce such qualities as will make it void of offence to the more cultivated eye, so much the better; but the particular aim and intention must be paramount. In like manner, if the illustration be for purely ornamental purposes, or purely pictorial, giving pleasure to the eye and the sense of beauty: then to attempt to make it fulfil the function of a teacher, to anything more than a subordinate degree, is to divide, and therefore to weaken, both capacities.

An illustration, therefore, should be thought out, designed, and produced, with a definite and single purpose.

Speaking of the rise and development of newspaper illustration, in a lecture delivered before the Society of Arts, in November, 1893, Mr. Henry Blackburn quoted from a discussion held at the same place in 1875, when the following conclusion was arrived at: "In the production of illustrations we have arrived at great proficiency, and from London are issued the best illustrated newspapers in the world. But our artistic skill has led us into temptation, and by degrees engendered a habit of making pictures when we ought to be recording facts. We have thus, through our cleverness, created a fashion, and a demand from the public, for something which is often elaborately untrue.

"Would it, then, be too much to ask those who cater for (and really create) the public taste, that they should give us one of two things, or rather *two things*, in our illustrated papers—the real and the ideal.

"1st. Pictorial records of events in the simplest and truest manner possible."

"2nd. Pictures of the highest class that can be printed in a newspaper."

This, it appears, was said before the mechanical process block was much used or even known; but what was true in principle in the old wood-engraving days is as true now that we have new and rapid means of reproduction.

Having, in any given case, decided what is the purpose of the illustration required, it will next be necessary to determine by which of the methods at our disposal the scheme can best be carried out, both as regards the method of producing the original, and the method of reproducing it in print. And this naturally brings us to the subject of our next chapter.

CHAPTER IV.

REPRODUCTION BY HALF-TONE PROCESS.

From the processes with which I propose to engage my reader's attention, wood and steel engraving, and kindred methods, stand apart.

Were we dependent upon these alone, not one-thousandth part of the illustration matter of to-day could ever have been produced, encumbered as the older methods are with the two things which, in the production of anything "for the million," are serious drawbacks, namely, time and expense of production.

Whilst these older methods undoubtedly possess characteristics which will always give them a peculiar value, and secure for them immunity from extermination (and make them, indeed, essential for certain purposes), there was long ago felt a need for a method of rapid reproduction unattended with individual artistic skill on the part of each worker employed, and, above all, free from heavy expense. Such a need has been more than met by what we now know as the mechanical processes. I say more than met, because, gradual improvement in the processes themselves, and an increased knowledge of the particular requirements of these processes on the part of the draughtsmen or artists, has resulted in giving us a process which is not only rapid and cheap, but which produces prints of high quality and merit.

It will of course be at once apparent that in order to get our illustration into the printed pages of book or newspaper we must first transfer the original to a plate, or block, and then so manipulate the surface that, like a printer's type, it shall take the printing ink in such manner as shall leave an exact imprint upon the paper, or other surface, upon which it is pressed.

The transfer of the original is accomplished by photography. The preparation of the surface is effected by a chemical or mechanical process. Correctly defined, these processes are "photo-mechanical," and such are generally understood by the literally ambiguous title "process," which is colloquially applied to all such methods.

It is not the intention of the present book to give instructions whereby to work the processes, beyond a general outline which shall make the illustrator acquainted with the method in which his drawing or photogram is utilised. This knowledge will enable him, to some extent, to adapt himself and his work to its special requirements.

Photo-mechanical processes are of two kinds: those by which the image is *ingraved*, known as *intaglio*, and those in which the image is produced in *relief*, or *relievo*. In the first of these the result is more or less similar to an ordinary engraved copper-plate, which, being wiped after inking, retains the ink in the engraved or indented portions, and prints accordingly. The intaglio processes are confined to what is known as Photogravure, or Photo-etching, and modifications thereof. This will not engage our attention, for, beautiful as are its results, it is comparatively expensive, and lacks that characteristic of speed which has made the *relief* processes so useful. The engraved plate must be printed *separately*; it cannot be set up with type and printed as letterpress. At the same time, in order to clear my reader's mind, and my own course, before proceeding further, mention may be made of other separate-printing processes, such as Collotype[1] (also known under many fancy titles), in which the image is printed on a machine or press from an inked gelatine surface. These can easily be distinguished by the image having a perfectly even appearance as though produced by a water-colour wash, without grain, reticulation, or lines. Photo-lithography, in which, as the name implies, the picture is transferred on to stone, from which it is then printed as in ordinary lithography, may also be mentioned here.

**HALF-TONE FROM PHOTOGRAM; HIGH LIGHTS
STRENGTHENED WITH CHINESE WHITE.**

Another beautiful process of reproduction is the Woodbury-type, named after its inventor, Walter B. Woodbury, in which a bichromated gelatine film is exposed under a negative, and the soluble portions afterwards removed by hot water. The resulting gelatine relief, which contains a facsimile picture, is allowed to dry, when it becomes as hard as stone. It is next forced by hydraulic pressure into a sheet of polished lead, leaving therein an exact counterpart of its every elevation and depression. The lead plate (*intaglio*) is next placed in a handpress, and flowed with a pool of hot gelatinous colour; a piece of paper is next placed on top and pressure applied, when all surplus colour oozes from the sides. After a few moments, when the gelatine becomes sufficiently cool, the paper bearing its delicate gelatine print is pulled off and dried.

LINE REPRODUCTION FROM PEN AND INK.

*(Original 14 x 11 inches.)*LINE REPRODUCTION FROM PEN AND INK.

Beautiful as many of these are, they can only be applied where the expense attending them and the slower printing is not an objection, and where letterpress is not required on the same sheet at the same printing. Printing matter can of course be afterwards introduced, but this must be by a second operation.

We have now left for consideration the relief processes, in which the design to be printed is produced similar in character and appearance to that of the movable letterpress type used by printers.

FEEDING THE CHICKENS.

(Half-tone from photogram. Original 14 x 11 inches.)

These processes are roughly divisible into two sections, "tone" and "line," to understand which I will refer the reader to the accompanying illustrations.

In these the image appears to be respectively composed of *lines* of varying strength and proximity in the one, and of *tints* ranging from grey to black in the other. If the latter be closely examined, however, or looked at through a magnifying glass, it will be found that what at first appears to be a flat even tint is composed of an infinite number of dots arranged in a reticulated or geometrical pattern. We will now see how this effect is produced, and what are the especial uses of this so-called "tone" or "half-tone" process.

THE HERON HOUSE.

Half-tone from photogram. (Original 14 x 11 inches.)

HALF-TONE PROCESS.

As has been already said, it is of course necessary to produce from the original a printing surface of such a kind as shall take ink and print an image therefrom. Now it will of course be obvious that with ink and white paper we can only produce two things—black and white—and that therefore all the intermediate shades must be produced by a greater or less number of black dots. The process under consideration, in common with some others, is based upon the fact that gelatine or albumen sensitised with bichromate of ammonium or potassium, becomes *insoluble* after being acted upon by light. A solution of bitumen in benzole also forms a light sensitive coating which is frequently used in these processes. If we were to expose such a sensitive film to light under (for example) a photographic negative of a figure taken against a light background and then washed it in a suitable solvent, those parts which had been protected from light by the opaque portions of the negative, such as the background, the face, hands, and white portions of the dress, would dissolve away, leaving the insoluble or light affected portions standing.

LINE REPRODUCTION FROM PEN AND INK.

(Original 14 x 11 inches.)

If we were now to ink these portions, we could print a black image which would represent the general form of the portrait like the old-fashioned silhouettes, or shadow pictures; but the "half-tone" process provides for the breaking up of the solid black image, substituting for it black dots closer and more numerous where the darker greys are, and less so where the shading is lighter. A very considerable variation in apparent tint may thus be effected.

The actual method is briefly thus:—What is known as a "screen" is first made by taking a photographic negative of a print from a copper-plate, on which has been ruled about 120 fine parallel lines to the inch. This is done with extreme care and exactness, so that the negative gives a clear transparent copy of the ruled lines of microscopic sharpness. In many cases the ruled copy is moved round a quarter of a circle during the exposure, thus resulting in the effect of double ruling, the lines intersecting each other at right angles. Or two printings may be made from the copper-plate to produce the same result and the negative then taken. We shall thus have a negative having the appearance of a very fine lattice of transparent glass on an opaque ground.

With this "screen" placed nearly in contact with an ordinary photographic plate, film to film, we proceed to make a copy negative, in the camera, of the original picture. This, when developed, will give the picture *and* an image of the screen, which has been interposed, together on one plate.

If this is now clear to my readers, they will probably at once see what will result when such a plate is used on a sensitised sheet of zinc or copper, and the soluble parts of the film washed away as before suggested.

The parts of the film made insoluble from exposure to light will be reticulated all over by minute soluble dots or lines where the image of the screen has interrupted the light, and more so or less in proportion to the lightness or deeper shade of the original, and by this means what would have been unbroken blacks are sprinkled over, so to speak, with tiny white interstices, the ink when applied remaining on the alternating projections of undissolved film.

Suppose the film to have been of bitumen and spread upon a sheet of zinc, we should have a reticulated image in insoluble bitumen with interstices of plain zinc. This bitumen forms a protective coating, so that when immersed in a weak solution of nitric acid the acid only eats a way into the bare metal. Gradually, and by subsequent acid baths, the parts covered by the film are left in strong relief, and in a fit condition to print from. The film which has thus resisted the acid is then washed away, leaving the zinc relief.

To carry out the above process many details, which I have not thought it the office of this book to enter into, will be required. Thus the solvent used for developing, or, in other words, washing away the soluble portions of a bitumen film, is turpentine; but water is used in the case of bichromatised albumen. An acid resisting preparation is finally applied to the plain zinc relief, and the whole block re-etched or "re-bitten," so as to strengthen the image; certain precautions, moreover, are taken to prevent the acid "under etching" the image—and a great deal more which, of course, would have to be clearly described were it intended to teach the process of block-making.

In the variety of half-tone blocks, known as Typogravure, a different method of breaking up the surface is adopted; no intervening screen is used, but the surface of the metal has imparted to it a preliminary roughness or grain, and the image is printed and etched on this rough surface. These blocks, when carefully printed from, yield exceedingly nice results, the grain having something of an "aquatint" character, which appears to be more discriminating than that derived through the use of the ruled screen. The softness of outline and freedom from anything like a mechanical texture is well seen in blocks made by this method. The remarkable difference obtained from the same block by different printers will at once suggest that a very great deal depends upon the printing quite irrespective of the quality of the block itself. Many letterpress printers make a specialty of block-printing, the chief art being in the "making-ready" and "underlaying," by which terms is understood the careful adjusting of the block, so that its surface be at exactly the proper elevation to secure the proper amount of pressure, neither more nor less, when on the printing machine. Some further remarks on this subject will be found in Chapter X.

UNTOUCHED HALF-TONE FROM PHOTOGRAM.

(Original 4 x 3.)

I trust, however, enough has been said to give a general idea to the uninitiated of how we arrive at the dotted ink print, which we recognise as a reproduction from a photogram, or wash-drawing, or indeed anything which is similarly made up of flat tints.

HALF-TONE FROM PHOTOGRAM—THE BLOCK ENGRAVED ON BY HAND.

(Original 4 x 3.)

It will, of course, have been understood that the ruled "screen," which is interposed between the picture to be copied and the plate on which it is copied, will appear over *the whole* of the copy negative, whether the image extend so far or not, so that, in the reproduction, even what should be blank whites will be covered with the fine black dots or grain, though more widely separated by little white spaces.

ON SLAPTON LEY, SOUTH DEVON.

Photogram touched up by hand—block untouched.

(Original 4 x 3.)

If the accompanying reproductions be examined, this will be found to be the case.

To any one who has given pictorial matters much thought, the disadvantage of this will be at once apparent.

In black-and-white pictures, white is the highest expression of light, and yet how far the whitest paper is from sunlight, and how much shorter the whole gamut of tones, from blackest ink to whitest paper, is when compared with the scale of Nature, have often been pointed out and are now generally understood. But our half-tone process makes the range of tones still shorter by curtailing it at the top of the scale and cutting off the white: the pervading "tint," or "grain," reducing white to a light grey, and not even the deepest blacks and intermediate tones are nicely rendered except by very careful printing. The printing of half-tone process blocks has received great attention amongst better-class printers of late, with the result that marked improvement has taken place, and it is clearly seen that be a half-tone block ever so well made it is only admirable when special ink and special paper (notably a fine clay surface paper) are used, and more than ordinary knowledge and care expended in the machining.

While the ideal process block is one in which, when the process is completed, the block is ready for the press (and many process houses pride themselves upon turning out "untouched" blocks), yet there are few houses who do not employ some hands who are constantly working with engraver's tools to "improve" the blocks after the last etching is done.

Much brilliancy of contrast and effect may be accomplished if the engraver cut away the grain altogether on that part of the surface of the block where it should print white; but this must necessarily be done by men of instinctive taste and good judgment, for immediately hand carving be admitted the essential character of an *automatic facsimile* process is lost. The illustrator or artist will, therefore, unless he give careful and precise instruction as to what parts are to be cut away, or can superintend the work himself, feel considerable hesitation in entrusting such a delicate task to a stranger. One little touch in the wrong place, one bit of plain white too many, and the harmony of the whole illustration will be upset; so that many will reasonably prefer a weak flat print to the uncertainty which must attend the leaving of a block to a mechanic's mercies.

In the accompanying three illustrations we have, first, an untouched "half-tone" block from an ordinary photogram; secondly, a block from the same original, "fine etched" or with the etching controlled so as to brighten the effect; and thirdly, a block made from the same photogram which, in order to compensate for any failings of the process, has been worked on *by the artist*, strengthening the shadows and brightening the lights.

This brings us to consider the subject of working on photograms by hand, and the preparation of illustrations generally, which is dealt with in a separate chapter.

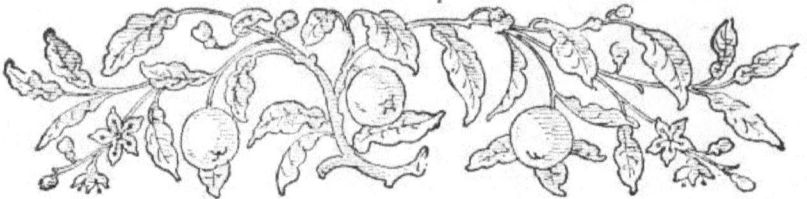

CHAPTER V.

THE PREPARATION OF ORIGINALS FOR REPRODUCTION BY HALF-TONE PROCESS.

I. PHOTOGRAMS.

It will be understood from the foregoing chapter that in every case where the original to be reproduced is of such a nature that before a print in ink can be made the image must be broken up, the reproduction will have to be effected by means of the half-tone process.

Of the various kinds of originals thus utilised, probably the two most common are photograms and wash-drawings.

The rapidity, comparative ease, and absence of the draughtsman's skill, with which photograms can now be made, has placed a wonderful power in the hands of author or illustrator. But a short series of photograms of some subject of interest with a very little descriptive letterpress will often form an acceptable contribution to magazine or newspaper, and yet a thoughtful consideration of such illustrations can hardly fail to impress any one with the drawbacks and defects of the method.

Such illustrations too often strike us as dull, misty, grey, and lacking brilliancy, when compared with black and white reproductions of another kind.

This dulness is attributable to a great extent to the gauze-like screen through which the copy is made, as described in our last chapter. The bright lights are grained over with fine dots reducing white to grey, and the soft finely graduated half-tones are often lost altogether.

In order to counteract these defects, the process worker will often take upon himself to "doctor" the negative made from the original before proceeding to make the block, a practice to be condemned because such an operator is rarely possessed of artistic judgment, and his "touching up" may often produce a result unexpected and unacceptable to the artist.

A similar "touching up" may also be effected on the block itself, as previously suggested, which is only preferable because the artist may more directly control the engraver's tool by giving definite instructions.

As far as possible, however, the block should not be meddled with by any one, if the originals have been produced in such a manner as to ensure the best possible effect by the mere mechanical process.

In making photograms especially for reproduction a clear, bright negative, with good strong contrasts, should be aimed at. Probably the kind of negatives which it was customary to strive after in the older days of wet-plate photography would be the best; but, as wet-plate photography is hardly practicable for the illustrator of to-day, similar results with dry-plates should be sought.

Unhappily, the extreme softness and exquisite gradations of some of the most modern and artistic work of photographers is thrown away in the process of reproduction, and little more than a flat, meaningless smudge is the best the process block can make of it. For this reason our photograms for illustration should somewhat exaggerate the effect we wish to reproduce: a matter which has led to the working on photograms with the brush to heighten the effect, of which I shall have more to say anon.

Given the proper kind of negative the next care will be to make such a photographic print as shall not detract from the qualities secured in the negative, and shall in every possible way assist the "process."

Many of the best and most pleasing photograms of our day are printed upon coarse-grained, rough-surfaced paper, presenting a difficulty to the reproductive process almost certain to prove disastrous to the result; for if, whilst being copied, the original is not very skilfully lighted, the inequalities of the surface reproduce as little lights and shadows in a very unpleasing manner, and the texture of even a comparatively smooth paper seems remarkably exaggerated.

Almost as undesirable will be the very highly enamelled surfaces of some photographic papers, the surface gloss producing reflections which interfere with the copying. The best for general use will be the smoothest platinotype paper, or a not too highly-glazed *white* albumenised paper, either of which are obtainable at most chemists and all photographic dealers. The print should be of a medium depth, not so dark as to give heavy solid shadows, nor so light as to omit all detail from the lightest portions. The various manipulations necessary for "toning" and "fixing" the print should be carried out carefully, especially avoiding staining or discoloration of the white paper. The print thus made, when mounted on card, is as far as an ordinary photogram can go for this purpose.

It now remains to be seen, bearing in mind what we know of the method by which it is to be reproduced, what may be done to improve it, never forgetting, however, that the chief value of a photogram for illustrative purposes is its unimpeachable fidelity to truth. Additional hand-work should not violate this truthfulness by the introduction of any fresh matter, or the painting out of any characteristic detail, unless, of course, the illustration is merely for pictorial or decorative purposes. The inscription "From a photogram" usually possesses a charm over the popular mind, inspiring confidence and carrying conviction, and if the hand-work be discreetly introduced, only to improve the effect and counteract the inherent defects of the final process, the legend may be honestly used.

In the first place, a photogram in which there are some large very dark objects, which by reason of their dark colour are disagreeably heavy, or obtrusive masses of deep shadow, may be made to reproduce better if a thin transparent wash of blue be applied to such portions. The great photogenic power of blue is, of course, the reason of this, but until some experience be gained as to the proper amount of blue required, I should recommend that a duplicate untouched photogram be sent in as well, with a few words of explanation and instruction to the process man. If the photogram be upon a glossy surface paper, a few drops of ox gall, procurable in bottles from the artists' colourman, will make the water-colour wash flow readily over the slimy surface.

For working with a brush upon the photogram, the materials are simple and few. Our purpose is to strengthen the lights and deepen the darks, for which purpose Chinese white and two or three water-colours respectively will be used.

The surface and general character of a platinotype or matt paper print will be pleasantest to work on; with an albumenised paper, ox gall will again be essential.

If a liberal amount of hand-work is intended, the print had better be a light one, and it can then be built up to any degree.

Chinese white, when applied thinly, has a bluish hue, and will consequently reproduce somewhat lighter than it appears. Therefore to produce a grey, it will sometimes be better, instead of using thin Chinese white, to make an admixture of Chinese white and Indian ink, or some suitable pigment, and apply it as a grey where grey is wanted. Such portions of the Chinese white which, when dry, appear harsh, may be softened with a clean almost dry sable brush; or the soft part of the finger, with little more than its natural moisture, carefully rubbed over the harsh parts may have the desired effect. By such and any tricks which may suggest themselves it is advisable to blend the hand-work with the actual photographic image.

In applying pigment to the dark parts, to make them darker or sharper, it will be desirable to match the colour of the photographic print as nearly as possible. With platinotypes this may easily be done with Indian ink, with a little blue added according to whether the print is a warm or cold black. The precise colour of a silver print, whether on matt or albumenised paper, is not so easy to match, but may be best accomplished with sepia and cobalt, with a trace of crimson lake; one or two other colours, such as burnt umber, vandyke brown, sienna, &c., being kept in reserve for emergencies. Fine-pointed small sable-hair brushes will be found the best for all purposes.

"STOPPED OUT" PHOTOGRAM.

(*Original 6 x 4.*)

In the process of reproduction the original may be enlarged upon or reduced.

The former is not often attended with happy results, especially if there is much hand-work, but reduction may to some extent be relied on to clear away any trifling blemishes, should such exist. I should, however, lay emphasis upon making the original as perfect as possible; the "improving" effect of the process is an altogether too uncertain and unknown factor to be trusted.

Having thus given particulars as to the preparation of photograms for reproduction, we may now suggest some various applications thereof.

There is a great charm about illustrations which possess a spontaneous and a suggestive character, and in this direction photograms are too often painfully deficient. On rare occasions only, and in the hands of a few artistic workers alone, does photography rise above a certain mechanical and laboured impression, and the rare exceptions are of a character ill-suited for "half-tone" reproduction.

For complete whole-page illustrations a photogram has few drawbacks; but when inserted with letterpress, and required for chapter headings and odd corners, the fact that the picture occupies the whole space enclosed within the boundary lines, and includes a great deal of detail which is not required, makes them less attractive. Their form and style is dull and monotonous.

The accompanying illustration will suggest the manner in which I would recommend photograms to be sometimes employed—especially when the illustrator does not possess the requisite skill to produce the same thing with his brush.

The "Little Gate-keepers" may be taken as an example of what I will call a "stopped-out" photogram; practically no hand-work has been employed upon it beyond the "stopping out" of the original negative. The figures of the children holding open the gate appear in the foreground of a large negative, a landscape near Dunster Castle; the background is composed of trees of an unpleasing form, and, beyond the topographical interest, the bulk of the subject has little to recommend it.

The method of stopping-out is as follows:—The negative should be placed in such a position as to secure a strong transmitted light; it may be fastened to the window, so as to be able to look through it towards the sky, or may be placed in a retouching desk, as used by photographers, if very large plates. In my own practice I use an ordinary easel, sitting to it with my face to the window. On the film side of the negative carefully draw round the more critical outlines, such as figures, faces, trees, &c., with a very fine-pointed brush, or a pen, dipped in opaque black varnish, gradually broadening the line to about a quarter of an inch. Now on the reverse, or glass side of the negative, paint out with black varnish all the rest as required; the effect of painting-out on the reverse side being to give a slightly softer or vignetted effect as is seen in the ground and gate-posts of the accompanying illustration.

Where it is desired to carry the vignetted effect to a greater length, some oil colour, red by preference (which may be thinned with copal varnish), may be used, and when partially dry the finger may be used as a dabber to remove just sufficient to admit of the plate printing very faintly.

In such a practice as this a little resourcefulness and ingenuity will stand the operator in good stead, and many modifications and "dodges" will occur as the work proceeds. Thus, for instance, if the whole of the painting out be done on the film side, the bare outline of the background and surroundings may be scratched in with a needle so as to give a sketchy appearance in the print; such sketched outline may adhere to the original form or may be entirely invented. Some taste must be exercised to prevent the elaborate photographic image from appearing incongruous with the sketched outline.

In the accompanying "Boy gathering Wortleberries," two children have been taken out of an unfortunately grouped trio, a badly developed transparent sky has been converted into a hill in the background, and some little details of landscape have been painted on to the print.

A good deal has been said of the modern illustrator shirking or ignoring backgrounds in his illustrations, yet I am inclined to think that in such cases as these, and very many others, the background is best only suggested or omitted altogether. In an illustration which purposes to tell us some little fact, or is designed to beautify and enliven a page, we do not want a whole chapter from nature's book, but just such selected passages which the judgment of the artist illustrator shall select.

In utilising photograms in this or any similar manner, it is difficult to place such methods in the hands of those unlearned in art matters without a word of caution and advice on the subject of composition and arrangement; but as it is not within the province of the present work to instruct my readers in art principles, such remarks must be of the briefest.

It will be at once seen that whatever be the arrangement or "composition" of nature (as photographed), as soon as the illustrator commences stopping-out certain portions, the form or composition is at once entirely under his control, and the pleasing effect of the finished result will very greatly depend upon a nice arrangement of lines. Thus in my "Little Gate-keepers" the upper outline of the gate forms a striking line running obliquely upward from left to right, and so, to counteract this, I have let the ground take an oblique form in an opposite direction. To have done otherwise and repeated the first-named line would have given the whole thing a one-sided, running-upwards, effect. As a general rule (subject, as all such rules must be, to numerous exceptions), strong oblique lines should converge towards an imaginary centre some distance outside the picture, with some lesser opposing lines to form contrast and promote a balance. Neither should the sketched-in or created background repeat the form of the chief object. Thus in the "Boy gathering Wortleberries" the figure forms a vertical line; there are no strong oblique lines, and therefore the middle distance takes the form of a horizontal line. The summit of the hill, had it come directly over the boy's head, would have too evidently repeated his outline, and is therefore placed a little to the right. These are matters of taste, rather than the obedience to prescribed rules, but the reader who desires guidance can hardly do better than read Burnett's "Essays on Art." There are several handbooks to artistic photography which treat of this subject, such as "Pictorial Effect in Photography" and "Picture-making by Photography," both by H.P. Robinson; also "Studies in Photography," by J. Andrews; and many books for the art student.

Boy gathering Wortleberries -- Exmoor

WORKED-UP PHOTOGRAM.
(*Original 6 x 4.*)

But, as already said, these are matters of individual taste and artistic instinct, and although I hope by this little book to make the path easy for those who have no especial artistic aptitude, yet, in such things as this, the possessor of such instinctive sense of form is at an advantage, lacking which the attentive study of other people's work and some amount of imitation seems to be the only possible substitute. Much knowledge may be gained from analysing, to this end, illustrations which greet the eye on nearly every page of current literature. While many methods of illustration *may* be learned and practised in a mechanical manner, the course is beset with difficulties and pitfalls, and, to the artistically unlearned, the alternative dangers of gross error and sheer imitation are ever present. Mr. Henry Blackburn has justly said, "The illustrator's best protection against this tendency, his whole armour and coat of mail, is to be an artist first and an illustrator afterwards." Yet men have won battles without armour, and when the stripling slew the giant it was the latter who wore the coat of mail. Zeal and patient application will do much.

In speaking of the application of the photogram to illustrative and decorative purposes, we can hardly leave the subject without making reference to the use to which they may be put for decorative initials, chapter headings, and the like. Some very excellent examples of initials were given in Mr. Gleeson White's articles on "Photographing the Nude," published in *The Photogram*, one of which we reproduce (see p. 48). The subject must be selected so as to harmonise in character and form with the letter required, and such letter may then be pasted, or painted, on the original negative, in which case it will print white; or it may be worked on the photogram with brush and pigment. In only a few cases would the initial, if represented in deep black, have any other than an overpowering and heavy effect. The "tail-piece" on page 56 is a further example which needs little explanation. Photograms cut to certain form, and arranged suitably, may make a great variety of chapter headings or tail-pieces.

In the example here given, the background or distance was painted out on the negative, and ink lines were drawn around the print before reproduction.

In order to ensure a symmetrical and sharp outline, a paper mask may be attached to the negative, and a scroll design painted on the negative, details being drawn in ink on the resulting print.

THE BATTLE OF ALEXANDRIA; 42ND HIGHLANDERS GUARDING FRENCH PRISONERS.

By permission of the proprietors of "The Illustrated London News." Engraved from a wash drawing in black and white by The Meisenbach Co., Ltd., West Norwood.

CHAPTER VI.

THE PREPARATION OF ORIGINALS FOR HALF-TONE REPRODUCTION.

II. Wash Drawings, Oil Paintings, Pencil and Other Drawings.

OF the remaining methods, whereby originals for reproduction by half-tone process may be made, much less need be said. The same principles of avoiding too fine and delicate gradations of tone apply as when making a simple photogram, and the methods of brush and pencil appeal almost exclusively to the naturally artistic.

The wash drawing, which is practically water-colour painting in monochrome, is the most popular, and, in the hands of those artists who have applied themselves to illustration for photo-reproduction, some very wonderful achievements are possible. Avoiding blue, green, red, orange, or colours approaching thereto, it matters little what colour is used, but probably black, such as Indian ink, or a good neutral grey or sepia, is the best to use. In any case, body colour reproduces better than transparent washes, the delicacy of which are wasted. Hence a liberal use of Chinese white to lighten the tints is preferable to making the colour thinner with water. Lamp black and Chinese white work well together and reproduce excellently. In using Indian ink, or indeed any colour, successive washes should not be made until each preceding one is dry, thereby escaping a "messy" effect and securing greater vigour.

The brush-work must be bold and strong, and, as was said with regard to photograms, include as little of the softer half-tones as possible, the contrasts of light and shade must be accentuated and effect exaggerated to compensate for the degradation of contrast brought about by the process. Unless this be remembered, the result can hardly fail to give anything but a very flat poor copy of the original. The artist should hold himself under restraint, and instead of blending one tone with another keep them nicely distinct, limiting himself to some half-dozen different shades or tones between the extremes of white and black, and even then some portions of the white may require to be cut away on the block.

Many illustrations from wash drawings of to-day are of a daring, spirited style in which figures are drawn with or without backgrounds, and when *well* done they are undeniably attractive, and may be abundantly met with in such publications as *The Graphic, Illustrated London News, Sketch, In Town, St. Paul's*, and many others. Were we considering the subject of art in illustrations, comment on this sort of work not wholly in approbation might be made, but that it is thoroughly up to date, effective, and in ready demand cannot be denied, and it should be carefully studied by the student, who will no doubt profit by the suggestions of technique without necessarily copying or being unduly influenced by the style.

Some capital effects may be obtained by making a wash drawing on grey-tinted paper and putting in the lights with white, an example of which is here given. Decorative designs done in Chinese white on dark-brown paper may be successfully produced, but should be made several times larger than required; the reduction in size usually improving the effect.

Painting in oil in monochrome will offer a welcome field for illustration work to those who are more accustomed to use this medium. A smooth surface canvas or board should be chosen, however, and the painting should be smooth, all *strong* brush marks, especially in the whites, being omitted or softened out with a badger. In thus softening, however, care should be exercised not to graduate one tone into another, but leave everything firm and distinct, the same restriction of tones being observed as in the other methods referred to previously. In using oil colours, turpentine must be liberally used, or benzine, as this will destroy the excessive gloss on the surface, a feature not liked by the process worker.

ON THE RIVER ROTHER.

Half-tone from Indian-ink wash drawing on grey paper. (Original 5⅝ x 3⅞.)

Either water colour or oil may be worked upon a photographic basis in order to save labour or difficulties in drawing. In such cases the photographic print should be as faint as possible; any photographic paper may be used for water colour, but smooth platinotype will probably be the most pleasant. The surfaces to which oil colour may be applied will be naturally more limited, but ready-sized canvas for printing in bromide by artificial light is made, and is largely used for oil painting for the commoner kind of portraits.

**DESIGN—CHINESE WHITE ON ORDINARY BROWN PAPER—
HALF-TONE.**

(Original 7¼ x 4¾.)

It will, however, sometimes be found desirable to economise labour by using a photogram to paint on, thus saving time in re-drawing and ensuring accuracy of elaborate details. Moreover, paint may be put upon a photogram, and much matter that is not required, or which may be judged as injurious to the pictorial effect, can be omitted. After the painting is finished, the photographic basis or original will then require to be removed.

Almost any photographic print may be prepared to receive oil paint by giving it a coating of common "size," and drying it *slowly* by a fire or otherwise. The painting-on being then proceeded with, and the paint dry, the *back* of the print is to be sponged or brushed with the iodine solution mentioned on page 114. Platinotype paper being already sized requires no further sizing, and by making a weak under-exposed print the subsequent reduction or bleaching of the image can be rendered unnecessary.

By permission of the proprietors of "The English Illustrated Magazine".
Engraved from pencil sketch by The Meisenbach Co., Ltd.,
West Norwood.

Many illustrators are fond of making wash drawings and then strengthening them with pen or pencil. The advantage is not easy to see, a mixed and indifferent character being usually felt.

Pencil drawing with a reinforcement of a few ink lines, or pencil by itself, is a method which appears to me to be deserving of much more attention and cultivation than it has usually received.

EVENING AT WEST MERSEA.

Half-tone from pencil drawing. (Original 4½ x 3½.)

Average pencil drawing is inclined to be too weak, and wanting in those characteristics which have been already pointed out as essential in wash drawings, but if the drawing be vigorous, and the pencil strokes clean and distinct, some capital results may be obtained. In order to procure the grey of pencil work a very fine screen is used, and the printing carefully attended to, so that pencil sketches are hardly suitable for the cheaper and more rapid class of printing. The lights should be cut away on the block.

The accompanying sketch of a cottage is simply torn from the leaf of a sketch-book in which it was made without any regard for the requirements of the process; the strong shadows were slightly reinforced with pen and ink, and the whole carefully reproduced.

COTTAGE AT HERONGATE.

Half-tone from pencil sketch slightly strengthened with pen and ink.

(Original 4½ x 3½.)

It seems scarcely necessary to refer to the use of water colour and oil paintings in colour as illustrations, inasmuch as if produced for purposes of reproduction, colour would hardly be employed. Occasionally, however, one may require to make a photogram of a painting for some such purpose, in doing which it will be best to employ a professed photographer who is accustomed to copying, and this because the photographing of coloured objects possesses peculiar difficulties.

Plates known as "Isochromatic" are used, these having certain dyes mixed with the sensitive film which makes them more sensitive to the least active colours, such as reds and yellows, and in addition a stained film of gelatine or glass is introduced into the lens to further correct the action of the colours. Special care, too, in lighting the picture to be copied is requisite, some experts recommending the use of coloured reflectors.

If the greens, reds, and yellows are not very pronounced, or the effect is not greatly dependent upon blue and such hues which by reason of their great light activity photograph as white, a fair copy photogram may be produced under ordinary circumstances; but where any doubt exists, I should recommend that the work be done by an experienced operator.

Throughout the foregoing remarks on the half-tone process, it will have been gathered that its inherent defects constantly stand in the way of our giving it unqualified approval. A recent writer on the subject, Mr. C.G. Harper, says of half-tone process that it is "inconstant and for ever incapable of rendering wash drawings as well as the wood-engraver."

Be this as it may—and it may not be possible to gainsay it—each day sees such improvements made in the processes, that even before these sheets are in my reader's hands circumstances may require a change of opinion, and prejudices may have given way under the convincing influences of modern improvements.

We may now turn our attention to the more direct processes of reproducing in *line*, in which, more than in any other direction, the revolution which photography has brought about in the art of illustration is evident.

CHAPTER VII.

LINE PROCESS.

The methods of drawing for reproduction by, and in compliance with the requirements of, a line process, are numerous and varied. They include pen, pencil, and crayon, and modifications and combinations of all three.

The information which I shall give is intended chiefly for such as know little or nothing of the manner in which such illustrations should be produced. Having already mastered the primary methods, the more practised draughtsman, knowing what any special reproduction process requires, will, to some extent, invent his own methods and often resort to some "dodge" which may occur to him, thereby producing some delightful and original result.

In describing the half-tone process we found the necessity of having an image in relief of such a character that we could print from it in ink, hence the intervention of a ruled screen, which broke up the flat even tints of the original picture into minute dots. Line processes, as the term implies, are used to reproduce an illustration which, as in a pen and ink sketch, possesses no flat tints, and requires no screen, the actual lines being reproduced in relief and printed in facsimile.

It will, of course, be remembered that a mechanical process block can only produce in simple black and white: that is, it either reproduces a line, to print black, or omits it altogether; so that a line drawn in grey ink, and another in black, would each reproduce exactly the same, namely black. Whereas in wash drawing we were limited to a few varying tones, we are now restricted to two—white and black—and, as may be seen by looking at any good line drawing, various degrees of shade are produced by a multiplicity of lines in greater or less proximity and of varying thickness.

Before proceeding further, I will give an outline of the three principal processes used for producing drawing in line. These are the swelled gelatine, the albumen, and the bitumen processes;—other processes exist but are little practised, and offer no advantages over the above. The albumen and bitumen methods are processes of etching on zinc and familiarly known as "zinco" line process; not so the swelled gelatine, as will be seen from the following description of it. Gelatine of a hard variety is melted in water with the addition of a small quantity of sugar and chrome-alum, and is then spread evenly upon a perfectly clean glass plate. This gelatine film is, when required for use, sensitised by immersion in a solution of bichromate of potassium, methylated spirits, and water. The effect of this is to render the film, to some extent, insoluble where acted upon by light; or, more correctly speaking, non-absorbent when affected by light. A negative, made from the original to be reproduced, is placed in contact with the sensitised film and exposed to light. The film, which it will be remembered is resting upon a glass plate, is then placed in cold water, with the result that those parts which have been protected from light absorb water and swell up, leaving the non-absorbent parts, which represent the image, sunk in. When this operation has been carried far enough, a plaster of Paris cast is taken, and from this a wax mould is made, which is practically a duplicate of the gelatine mould from which the plaster cast was made. Into the wax mould copper is deposited, precisely as in ordinary electrotyping, thus giving us a copper relief from a gelatine or wax mould made direct from the original.[2] This process, while a favourite with the artist, is not so readily used by the process worker because it is somewhat expensive, the average cost of a block being from 9d. to 1s. 6d. per inch. But the results are very fine, especially when a drawing has been made in ignorance or regardless of the requirements of process reproduction.

The zinc etching processes, by which the great mass of newspaper blocks are made, are less regardful of delicacies of execution which the swelled gelatine often reproduces with astonishing fidelity.[3]

In the albumen process the sensitive film is composed of egg albumen, bichromate of ammonium or potassium, and water, which is spread upon a *zinc* plate. After exposure to light under the negative, the whole surface is inked over with transfer ink, and then immersed in cold water and gently rubbed. The ink will wash away from those portions which have been protected from light by the opaque portions of the negative, and will adhere to those affected by light. Thus on a bed of zinc we have an ink image on a substratum of albumen, the exact copy of the original. The zinc has now to be etched with acid.

With bitumen the procedure is somewhat similar. The bitumen is first treated with ether, which will dissolve out only those constituents which, not being sensitive to light, are not required. The residue is dissolved in benzole and spread upon a zinc plate, as with the albumen process. After exposure to light under the negative, the bitumen film is washed with turpentine, which takes away all except those portions acted upon by light. The film is next washed in water and placed in a very weak solution of nitric acid, which at once attacks those portions of the zinc unprotected by bitumen. If what now remains of the film be inked over we shall have, as in the last process, an ink image of the drawing on a zinc base, and the plate is now ready for etching.

The etching is performed by successive baths of diluted nitric acid, gum and powdered resin being applied to the plate after each etching, and heated so as to run down the sides of the ridges of metal (which at each successive etching bath are gradually growing deeper) until the "biting" or etching be considered deep enough. The ink and substratum of albumen or bitumen are then cleaned off with American potash, and the plate is finally washed. Rebiting, or still further etching, may be required before the zinc relief is ready to be mounted on a wood block "type high" for printing purposes.

As in the half-tone process, I do not pretend to have given working instructions, but only such general particulars as may interest the artist or draughtsman whose work is to be reproduced. For either of these processes the average cost is 4d. to 6d. per square inch, with a minimum charge of 5s. for a single block. Each process has its special uses and applications; the process craftsman (whom nothing delights so much as a sharp, brilliant line) will usually recommend the bitumen, but the albumen method will often give a more pleasing result. As a general rule, if your work is placed in good hands, the particular process to be used is best left to them to decide, and if a proof be submitted some little alterations may be suggested which can be carried out by an engraver.

In the subsequent pages of this book I shall make little reference to these processes; enough has been said, and they are no part of the draughtsman's business, only it will be well to keep in mind throughout such general particulars as have just been given.

Little has been said with reference to the negatives used in reproduction; but as the draughtsman who also possesses some knowledge of photography may be tempted to copy his work himself, it may be well to point out that the negative image must be as sharp as it is possible to get it. The most trifling deviation in focussing, unnoticeable in ordinary photography, will tell seriously in making a reproduction; moreover the kind of negative one may have learned to make for ordinary photographic purposes will not do here. The function of the negative is, it will be remembered, to protect certain portions of the film from light, and to freely admit light where the image is, hence the denser portions of the negative must be very nearly, if not absolutely, opaque, and the image as nearly transparent as possible; thus giving what photography proper has taught us to abhor—a black and white print. With ordinary plates, the required amount of density is not always easy to get, and special photo-mechanical plates are supplied by Mr. John Carbutt, of Wayne Junction, Philadelphia, Pa., which give the desired result. These plates are slow, thickly coated, and capable of giving great density, all of which are characteristics peculiarly suitable to the purpose. But in the end the process man will not thank you for saving him the trouble of making a negative; he is accustomed to make negatives of a certain kind, and very properly prefers to do this himself.

Not the least contributory towards a good reproduction is the power which reduction from the original places in our hands. When making the copy negative it is most usual to make it much smaller, or, inversely, the original drawing is made a good deal larger than it is required to appear (See Illustration on page 72). A somewhat ragged line of (say) one-eighth of an inch in width, would, if sufficiently reduced in size, come out as a fine line no thicker than a hair. Though reduction carried to such a degree would be impracticable, a drawing twelve inches by nine inches, reduced to eight by six, will usually be advantageous. Not only is a certain degree of coarseness and roughness thus removed, but the lines themselves become smoother and rounder; lines, however, which are very close together, are apt to close up into a solid mass, both from the reduction and because lines sometimes have a tendency to thicken in reproduction—a point to be guarded against when drawing.

If a drawing be examined through a simple double concave lens, that is to say the reverse of a magnifying-glass, the effect of reproduction can be seen, and the result anticipated; such lenses, called "diminishing glasses," are sold expressly for the purpose.

The reader need hardly be reminded that everything on the drawing will be reproduced, except perhaps *blue* pencil lines, this colour being photographically white; hence all finger-marks, spots, and stains must be carefully avoided. No doubt these, and sundry faults in drawing, can be cut away by the engraver, but an ideal block is one which requires no such helps to perfection, but which comes from the etcher's hands ready for use, and to such an ideal even the tyro must work.

The strong point and chief recommendation of a process block is that it reproduces in *facsimile* the draughtsman's original; once introduce hand-work and it begins to lose this character; moreover expense and delay in production are incurred, again depriving the mechanical block of its distinctive and valuable features.

Sundry elemental methods of getting an image on to zinc for etching without the intervention of photography may perhaps suggest themselves to the reader. Thus, for instance, an outline drawing may be made in transfer ink on transfer paper and at once laid down on the zinc and etched. A glass plate, coated with a soft opaque substance, may have a design scratched thereon and be used in place of a negative; but such methods are crude and limited, and need not be considered here.

We will now pass to an examination of the various kinds of drawings suitable for reproduction by relief process blocks, describing as nearly as possible how they are made and with what materials.

CHAPTER VIII.

METHODS OF LINE REPRODUCTION.

To those who have not previously given the matter attention, it will be a source of some astonishment to find a wide range of tones, that is varying degrees of light and shade, may be suggested by so simple and unpromising a means as black lines on a white ground. Perhaps no better means exists for getting some insight of this than by careful and persistent study of the line illustrations constantly appearing in the better class periodicals, such as *The English Illustrated*, *The Strand*, *Harper's*, *Sketch*, *Black and White*, and many others. In these we get frequent examples of the work of different men, and shall soon begin to realise not only the wide possibilities of line work, but the extremely different styles of various artists; and so long as the practice is not too long continued, or too much relied on, some advantageous exercise may be found in carefully copying such examples; being watchful in so doing that, quite independent of outline, our copy suggests the same materials, fabrics, &c., as are suggested in the original, and that this suggestion be arrived at by the same kind of treatment.

In this kind of drawing there is obviously no such thing actually as "tone," everything being black or white, and yet it is possible to suggest every gradation and most delicate tonal relationships of colours by this elementary means; the varied textures of objects can also be most convincingly suggested.[4]

Probably one of the first things that will strike us, on inspecting many styles of drawing, is the fact that while some draughtsmen expend enormous labour in filling the whole design with multitudinous strokes of the pen, others obtain effect by a very few lines and great expanses of white paper. A great number of strokes rapidly put in, in the manner of shading with pencil, and a few bold lines slowly and deliberately drawn, constitute the two chief differences of style. In the latter, the principal study is perhaps to know *what to leave out*, and nowhere is the knowledge and skill of the artist better seen than when the subject is satisfactorily rendered with the least possible amount of labour, there being not one unnecessary or superfluous line. Such powerful sketches, by Mr. Reginald Cleaver, may be seen in *The Daily Graphic*, and by Mr. Phil May in *The Sketch*. In these drawings a maximum of effect is attained with a minimum of work, and one feels that every line is essential and not one can be spared.

DRAWING BY MR. PHIL. MAY.

From "English Illustrated Magazine". An example of bold open drawing.

In most cases, for all the purposes of illustration, a black coat need not be suggested by any more lines of shading than a white gown; but the artist who so determines may carry his work to a higher standard and, with greater labour, even succeed in giving a suggestion of colour in the objects portrayed. But, even in such elaborate work, there should be no more execution than is essential, and the finished drawing should in no case make its elaborate execution felt. The thing which must first impress the spectator is the success of the general effect; never should there be first awakened a feeling of astonishment at the extraordinary amount of patience bestowed, or labour expended. If the first remark called forth is one of admiration for the extraordinary *dexterity*, we may be pretty sure that the draughtsman has been betrayed into the commonly besetting sin of over-elaboration, and whatever success has been attained in the effect rendered it would have been probably better if produced with less effort. It would have been more forcible if not overwhelmed, as it were, with so much work.

Never, then, let the delight which we may feel in making a pretty "finished" drawing get the better of our judgment when drawing for reproduction. Remember that "prettiness" comes very near to "pettiness," and delicacy and fineness are apt to become "niggling" and pedantic; coarseness is a lesser danger than excessive neatness.

Much of this, as already suggested, may be more clearly learned from the careful examination and comparison of good published drawings.

Imitate, and copy if you like, up to a certain degree, remembering always that you are thus copying merely *to ascertain by what means other men express their ideas in line, and not for your own practice.*

In like manner etchings, engravings, and indeed every kind of print made up of *lines*, may be studied and, to some extent, copied; but only in order to familiarise oneself with what lines, and combinations of lines, may be made to do; but the danger of continuing such a practice cannot be too much emphasised. Every artist or draughtsman, be he beginner or expert, must draw for himself and according to his own feelings and promptings. In every department of art the successful have had their imitators, and these again their imitators, and at each successive stage the further one gets from originality, the more trammelled, the more impotent and hopelessly beyond the possibility of really great work.

That the drawing is not the end in view, but merely a means to an end (that end being the reproduction), is a matter to which I shall refer later on; but it should here be noted, and moreover the student may be reminded, that every line and every mark which he makes will be *similarly reproduced* by the process. When drawing for wood engraving, the engraver could be instructed to strengthen this or leave out that; not so the mechanical block, which is to be regarded as normally an untouched and purely mechanical thing, only to be altered by hand on the rarest possible occasions, and then only when time and circumstances permit. This character of indiscriminating *facsimile* is not to be considered as a disadvantage in any way; the good draughtsman is thankful for it, he knows what to reckon upon, and to all it must be an incentive to do one's best. It is the same difference as between a mirror and an average photographer's portrait: the mirror may show us all our faults and yet, if we have any beauty, it does not belie us; while we know how often the ordinary commercial *carte-de-visite* is unreliable.

In the course of studying various reproductions we shall probably have become aware that the same things may be very differently rendered by different hands. Thus trees and foliage in landscape may be represented by an outline, and a few black patches and dots, or by numerous clearly drawn parallel lines, or yet again by irregular strokes crossing and recrossing each other; evidently, then, there is no intention here of *imitating* nature. And so, throughout, the aim of the pen draughtsman is to *suggest*, rather than to portray things exactly as they are. Lines, scratches, or dots, cannot pretend to imitate leafy foliage; and, be it noted, the same lines, scratches, or dots, may be similarly employed, in the same drawing, to suggest something quite different. It is in this employment of various pen marks, to suggest the composition of distinct objects, that individuality of style reveals itself; as does the discreet using of white blanks to express or suggest widely different things.

I have presumed throughout these pages that I may be addressing many to whom the idea of drawing in pen and ink (or other material) for reproduction, is entirely a new one; hence it will be necessary to examine the pen strokes which go to make up a complete drawing. Let it be well understood that many things are possible to the accomplished artist which must not be attempted by the beginner; later on we may learn, from our own experience, little freaks and tricks of our own, but we must first of all content ourselves with simple conscientious work.

In the following examples of pen and ink shading we have first the kind of strokes which the pen would make if used rapidly, as in writing, and without any particular care. In bold sketchy work this sort of handling may be permissible, but the student should practise shading by such lines as in No. 2. These are drawn rapidly in succession, the wrist being rested firmly on the table and the hand quite free, as in rapid writing. Commence at the top left-hand corner and work downwards; notice that each stroke is equidistant, parallel, and of the same thickness throughout its length. Look at this from a little distance and it appears like a grey, flat, even tint. This simple "shading" should be tried many times until perfect ease and certainty is acquired, each stroke of the pen being firm, distinct, and black; each stroke intended and nothing uncertain about it.

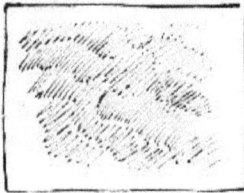

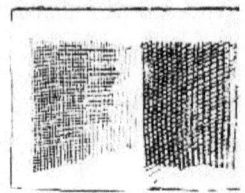

No. I.   No. II.   No. III.

EXAMPLES OF PEN AND INK SHADING.

Reduced to about half the size of original.

A good exercise will be to draw a square, and practise filling it with a flat tint consisting of lines either in the same direction, or else of lines in varying directions, and then with lines crossing each other or "cross-hatching."

Having now discovered how a flat tint may be laid down, and how such may be made uniformly or gradually darker, we may apply such methods to simple objects as the cube and vase here shown.

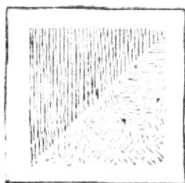

(Original 1½ x 1¼.)

By this time we may feel well on the road towards accomplishing any general subject which we are skilful enough to outline. Of the various mechanical helps to drawing outline, for those who lack the required skill, I shall speak hereafter.

(Original 4 x 2¼.)

It need hardly be pointed out that as there is, in nature, no such thing as

57

outline: it is purely an arbitrary means of indicating form, and separating one space from another; whether such spaces be occupied with shading or not, but especially where there is no shading.

At first it may perhaps be best to make a clear sharp outline of uniform thickness; but later we shall find we may often advantageously dispense entirely with outline, letting the shading only distinguish one object from another. Notice the absence of outline in the hills in "Near Berry Head," page 94.

A little experience will show us that an imperfect outline, and one which varies in thickness with various objects, will greatly assist in the attractiveness of our sketches. A too rigid outline, as also a too close adherence to what has been said about the precision of the shading strokes, tends to a stiff formal appearance which is not to be desired, and destroys anything like originality and individuality of style.

In the accompanying drawing notice these points—the irregularity of *outline*, in some parts its entire absence, the value of white spaces, and the suggestive little dots on the white foreground.

I have already remarked that the drawing is only to be regarded as a means to an end, and must therefore be made not so as to give satisfaction in itself, but so as to produce a good mechanical reproduction. However irksome some artists may feel this working for process reproduction, it is not accompanied with any great difficulties, nor are its special requirements so very restricting, if only we understand what is wanted.

Two influences, for good or for evil, exist between the original and the reproduction (two influences to be taken into account, and reckoned with when we are drawing, so as to produce a definite effect in the reproduction), and these are reduction and thickening of the lines.

A diminishing glass, used to examine any drawings, will at once show the effect of reduction or diminishing, and in rough and rapid drawing this reduction is depended upon to remove irregularities and coarseness.[5]

IN HARBOUR.
Pen drawing. (Original 7 x 6.)

It may be taken for granted that nearly every reproduction we see has been reduced from the original, some more, some less, and while generally speaking we may say that the effect of reduction is to refine and soften; the beginner, however, will sometimes be troubled by finding an increase in the thickness of the lines which is less agreeable, and is very fickle, and can only to a limited degree be counted upon as to the result. Hence the need for keeping darkly shaded portions as open as possible: that is to say, when lines are very close together, or there is cross-hatching, see that the lines do not needlessly run into each other, but that the little white interstices are well preserved. Keep the shading open (the rough net-like effect can be got rid of by reduction), and remember that not only do some lines thicken up, and so engulf the intervening white, but in reduction the white spaces reduce as well as the black lines, and may be reduced into invisibility.

Some definite rules have sometimes been suggested to guide the process man as to the amount of reduction best suited for average work; these, however, like many other rules of the kind, are quite arbitrary. On this subject Mr. Henry Blackburn says, with an authority based upon the experience of reducing, to various scales, some thousands of drawings: "As to the amount of reduction that a drawing will bear in reproduction, it cannot be sufficiently widely known that in spite of rules laid down there is no rule about it."

Same size as original.

In some instances no reduction is required, and the reproduction is so exact a replica of the original that it can hardly be distinguished, yet, "On the other hand, the value of reduction for certain styles of drawing can hardly be over-estimated"; and again, "Every drawing has its scale, to which it is best reduced."

The effect of the reduction may be seen in the accompanying three examples, the first being the same size as the original, and the others reduced as marked.

(Original 4¾ x 4¼.)

Until some experience has been gained in this direction, and apart from the exigencies of the space the illustration is required to fill, the process engraver will probably be the best authority for us to consult as regards the amount of reduction suitable to each individual drawing. A reduction of one-third is a very usual one, so long as the drawing is not unusually rough or clumsy.

Referring to the effect of reduction upon lines laid down to express a flat tint, Mr. H.R. Robertson gives some interesting notes upon the number of lines required to be drawn in an inch square to produce an even grey tint. I do not think too much importance should be attached to such calculations, as they are likely to embarrass the draughtsman and make him far too much concerned with the mere mechanism of his work; still, the matter is an interesting one. He says that from experiment he finds it will usually require about 108 to 120 lines within an inch to give to the naked eye the idea of a flat tint or wash, but that about 80 to an inch is as many as can be drawn to the inch by unaided vision; eighty lines to the inch gives 120 in 1½ inches, which, if reduced in reproduction by one-third, will give the requisite number of 120 to the inch which Mr. Robertson finds desirable. The effect produced, however, by parallel lines of shading alters considerably when the direction of the lines alters, and I think it is only necessary for us to glance through "Academy Notes," or any similar collection of sketches made by artists who understand the importance of conveying suggestions with pencil or pen, to assure us that far fewer lines are in many cases quite capable of giving the idea of an even tint. Such rules and figures are interesting, and perhaps useful, but they are certainly dangerous if the student places himself too much in subjection to their influence.

The beginner in pen drawing is probably destined to meet with severe disappointments at first from the manner in which the process will reproduce his work, and the inclination is to blame the process as unsympathetic, or the process man as incompetent, whereas the fault lies with the drawing, which is unsuitable through a want of proper regard for the requirements of process.

For instance, nothing is commoner with the student than to find such portions of our drawing as distance, sky, and the more delicate shading come up heavy and black—quite different to the original, and robbing such parts of it of all delicacy; or it may be that lines which we believed to be fine, smooth, flowing lines, reproduce as broken and irregular.

THE WILLOW HARVEST.
(*Original 7 x 14.*)

The root of both these evils will probably be found in the fact that in our drawing we have been producing light and distant effects by *grey* lines instead of fine black ones. Drawing with the pen insufficiently charged with ink, or with ink diluted with water, will give these grey lines; but the line process, recognising nothing but black and white, either reproduces the grey lines as black, or reproduces them imperfectly as broken and irregular. Here, then, will be another matter for the beginner to exercise himself in: namely, the drawing of good *black* lines and an avoidance of *grey* ones. With drawings made on a fairly large scale, so that every line can be made firmly and boldly, we are less likely to fall into making grey lines.

With etchings, in which the image is in intaglio, gradation in the lines is possible; because, according to the depth of the etched line, a greater or less amount of ink is contained, and a grey line can be printed therefrom. And so, for this reason, etchings are misleading if used as copies or examples from which to draw in pen and ink.

When the drawing has been first drawn in with pencil and inked over, every vestige of pencil marks must be carefully removed, otherwise the process reproduces them, not as soft grey marks, but as black as those made in ink, and some very unpleasant surprises will be the result.

CHAPTER IX.

TOOLS AND MATERIALS FOR LINE DRAWING.

To produce a line drawing which shall comprise such characteristics as have now been enunciated, three essentials will be required: a white surface, a black fluid, and a suitable instrument to convey the fluid at will. These we will take *seriatim*, in their conventional order—Papers, Inks, and Pens.

The material most largely used for drawing on is probably white Bristol board, of four-sheet or six-sheet thickness, and this will answer better than anything else in almost all cases. Some attention should be paid to the tint of the card, many cardboards having a tendency to turn yellow with age and exposure. A cardboard of a pure white, or a slight tendency to a bluish tint, is what we require, a blue card being in photographic reproduction practically the same as white. Upon the surface of the cardboard will greatly depend the ease with which we shall get clean sharp lines. With many cardboards, in which the surface is apparently smooth, the pen finds irregularities and sometimes obstacles to its smooth and even progress, catching and "spluttering" over little particles of hard matter or hair.

A good Bristol board, such as is procurable at any artists' colourman, presents no such difficulties, and the making of a fine smooth line should be quite easy. Messrs. Reynolds and Sons supply various kinds of boards equally suitable for pen work. The bank note Bristol manufactured by F.W. Devoe & Co. is also especially adapted to this work.

The process man will very likely recommend you to use a "clay surface" board, and no doubt in some instances these have their advantages. On these clay boards the pen strokes are remarkably clean and crisp, and have a good deal the appearance of having been produced mechanically rather than by hand; a very fine line, however, is difficult to produce, the result being rather like, but in a much less degree, drawing on an enamelled card on which the ink spreads; at the same time, however, there will be less liability to make grey lines. A further advantage of a clay surface is that the surface is easily removable with the blade of a penknife, so that faults may be scraped or cut away—a feature put to very important use in boards specially made for scraping, which are described on p. 96. For large, bold work a clay board is useful, but it should not be too often used on account of the hard, mechanical appearance of the drawing.

Whatman papers, or boards having a surface of Whatman paper, are also much used, and these are procurable in two surfaces: H.-P., or "Hot-pressed," the smoothest; and N., or *"Not* hot-pressed," the surface of which is sufficiently rough to make it very pleasant to work on, but not too much so. If using the H.-P., the surface must be wiped over with a clean wet sponge to remove a certain gloss which the process of hot-pressing imparts to it.

There is no particular virtue in any special paper or board beyond whiteness, evenness, and purity; any paper having these qualities may be used with success. I should not recommend the beginner to experiment with too many kinds; he will in the end be probably no nearer satisfaction than at the outset. Start on ordinary white Bristol and persevere, attributing failures to your own incompetence rather than to any fault in the materials. Some of the very best things have been produced on any scrap of notepaper or other white surface that has been at hand.

Of suitable black fluids there are many varieties, and the beginner may as easily concern himself a great deal too much about inks as about any other part of the necessary materials.

Cakes or sticks of dry pigment, or pans and tubes of moist colour, may be employed, but for general convenience a fluid black will be best. These are of two kinds: "fixed," which is not removable by water, and "ordinary"; and it may be well to consider beforehand the work we are going to do, and use the indelible, or fixed, ink if necessary.

I mean by this that we may sometimes require to use Chinese white over our black lines to produce whites, which could not easily be left as blanks, in which case it will be necessary to use a fixed black, else the Chinese white would smear and spoil the black.

The introduction of Chinese white is, however, an exception rather than the rule, and when the use of an indelible ink is not important, Stephens' Ebony Stain is admirable. It works easily, and although it dries with a slight gloss, which is usually a disadvantage, it reproduces well. It can be immediately thinned when becoming too thick by the addition of a little water, care being taken not to dilute it sufficiently to make it grey. It is sold in bottles at sixpence and a shilling, and is manufactured by the well-known makers of writing ink, but may be procured from the artists' colourmen. Messrs. Reeves and Sons have introduced a fluid black, called Artists' Black; this is made both "indelible" and "not indelible." This has become very popular of late, and is largely used; the not indelible, with water, making fine greys for wash drawing. Higgins' American "Waterproof" India Ink is also extensively used, and has received high commendation. Fixed Indian Ink is sold in fluid form, and Lampblack and Ivoryblack in tubes and cakes.

Ordinary writing ink is quite unsuitable; it "runs" when fine lines cross, and is either too blue or too brown in colour. Common Indian Ink is also too brown to reproduce well, so that the beginner will do wisely to use one of the above-named blacks, which are prepared for the purpose, and so diminish his chances of failure. All are sold in bottles at sixpence or one shilling.

Not taking account of eccentricities of accomplished artists, who may use some special medium to their fancy, and whose very mastership guarantees their success in whatever medium they may work, a dull intense black line on a pure white surface is the ideal to be attained.

It may be mentioned that if for any exceptional purpose the reproduction is to be printed in coloured ink, the original had better be drawn in a like colour, always excepting blue or anything approaching thereto. But brown, green, red, and orange are permissible, and will photograph correctly. A black drawing, reproduced in brown or other colour, is apt to give a very different impression, and still more so if a colour be reproduced in black.

Chinese white has been referred to, and should certainly always be at hand. If applied fairly thickly with a fine brush it will efface any faulty ink marks, and may also be used to introduce lights into shading which has been worked up too solid. It is also useful for putting in small lights, as in windows, or longitudinal white streaks on water which has been shaded in dark. It should be of good quality, and kept well stoppered in a strong glass or stone bottle.

With regard to the pen to be used there is more latitude for individual taste, as what one man can do with a given pen another cannot. The manufacturers who have given most attention to the requirements of draughtsmen are J. Gillott and Sons, the well-known makers of pens of all kinds. Many kinds of Brandauer's and Blanzy Poure and Co.'s pens are also very good.

It should not be supposed that a very fine-pointed pen is essential, for on the contrary a small tool often seems to lead to the making of small, niggling work. Mr. C.G. Harper finds a well-cut quill pen delightful for making pen studies, and says "it flies over all descriptions of paper, rough or smooth, without the least catching of fibres or spluttering. It is the freest and least trammelling of pens, and seems almost to draw of its own volition." A glass drawing-pen, such as is used by mechanical designers, &c., has its uses, but it is only capable of making a uniformly thick line.

An assortment of one dozen of Gillott's pens can be obtained for one shilling, and from these our selection can be made. Brandauer's No. 515 and No. 342 E.F. are well spoken of, and have the advantage of not becoming scratchy with use. A flexible pen, capable of making fine as well as thick strokes, working evenly, and not soon worn out, is what should be sought, and having found two or three kinds to suit, stick to them, and make yourself thoroughly master of their capabilities. Should any difficulty exist in obtaining a special pen, an ordinary "F" writing nib will not lead you far wrong, while for bold vigorous drawing I should prefer a gold "J"; it is clear from this that mere fineness of point is not an essential matter.

The possibilities of a particular pen are not learnt all at once, it should be persevered with and understood. It has been recommended that two or three pens of different character should respectively be used on different portions of the same drawing. There may be advantages in this, especially if a drawing contain a very wide variation in quality of its lines. It may sometimes be that very bold thick work in foreground is associated with fine delicate work in distance and sky.

Some artists prefer to use a fine brush instead of a pen. A small sable brush, having the outside hairs cut away, or a long hair brush known as "tracer" or "rigger," is capable of making fine lines hardly to be distinguished from pen strokes. At first they are slow to work with, but considerable rapidity may be acquired with practice. The lines are rounder and not so harsh as those made with the pen, and it is said that an artist who has once accustomed himself to use a brush never goes back to pens.

A FIELD PATH.

Bitumen process. (Original 7½ x 6½).

[See p.86.

The foregoing materials and pens are for the production of simple black line drawings on a white ground, and it is in this direction that I should advise the student to persevere and cultivate himself. All the beauty and expressiveness of lines is only realised after long practice; and, of the many ways of illustrating by line process, it is the best means of self-education, compared with which all others are flippant and inconsequent.

A FIELD PATH.

Swelled gelatine. (Original 7½ x 6½.)

[See p.86.

Still, with some truth it has been said that it is only by experiment that we learn to achieve distinction, and so after a while we may indulge in experiments in other directions, and try our hand at the various tricks which the ingenious have placed within our reach. These will be described in Chapter XI.

CHAPTER X.

COMPARISON OF PROCESSES.

The method of drawing in line referred to in the two preceding chapters may be regarded as traditional and of the normal character, and we shall next take under consideration various other methods of drawing equally suitable for reproduction by line process.

In the meantime, we will see how the processes for producing blocks in relief may be applied and see by a few examples how the results compare.

With the artist, the Swelled Gelatine process will probably rank as first favourite, and this because it is less exacting in its requirements.

Although only rendering the drawing in black and white, it is certainly more sympathetic, and does to some extent recognise the weaker impression of a grey line. By this process many ordinary black and white drawings, made without any regard for the demands of the process man, reproduce well, but would be impossible by the cheaper zinc etching; moreover, it is admirably suited to reproduce drawings in which a mixture of pen and pencil has been employed, an example of which will be given later.

]

MOONLIGHT.

Example of medium tint. (Original 4 x 7.)

The artist or draughtsman is not, however, usually master of the situation; the printer and publisher will use the cheaper methods, to suit which we must adopt, to a certain degree, a conventional manner. If a drawing be seriously studied, it is often surprising how much of the feeling of the draughtsman is conveyed to us through the strokes of his pen or pencil, and it is just this feeling which the Gelatine process preserves in great measure, but which the commoner methods sift out and give us a mere mechanical translation. Still, by suiting ourselves to these more ordinary processes, much may be done to compensate for the lack of sympathy which they display.

I have given (pp. 82, 83) two reproductions from the identical drawing, in order that comparison may be made.

The Bitumen process is characterised by the crude, sincere, line given, ignoring many finer lines, and bringing others up black and hard.

The Albumen process is the one by which probably the greatest number of blocks are made in this country, and, when carried to a high degree of perfection, yields some very pleasing results which, though inferior to swelled Gelatine, are better than the Bitumen. Ordinarily, however, there is not very much to choose between these two, and a very great number of examples would have to be examined in order to properly exhibit the differences.

PEN DRAWING.
Three different shading media. (Original 8 x 5¾.)

The comparison of results by these three processes is a subject which has given rise to some controversy. The artist, who has also usually been the author in this matter, has pronounced favourably for the swelled gelatine; but in this the process expert is in disagreement. After comparing carefully a variety of results, I am inclined to think that perhaps too much importance is attached to the supposed advantages of the swelled gelatine, and two powerful contributories to success are not sufficiently considered. Swelled gelatine is not used for ordinary newspaper work, and is charged at a much higher rate; and for this reason, probably, greater care is taken in the block-making, and, being used in higher class publications, it is more carefully printed from than is possible in the vast majority of cases when the cheaper blocks are used. The use of zinc blocks in cheap, rapidly printed publications probably prohibits the process having full justice done to it, and we are apt to judge its possibilities by the examples we too often see. Cheapness, short time, and rapid printing are factors calculated to spoil the reputation of any process. If bitumen and albumen could receive the same amount of care and attention as is customarily bestowed upon the more expensive swelled gelatine, there seems little reason why results should not be equal.

The River Wall near Rochford Essex —

UNTOUCHED LINE BLOCK.

(*Original 7 x 6.*)

In considering the application of such various methods, we are brought to that somewhat singular contest which seems to exist in every sphere of work wherein art is concerned, it is the disagreement and misunderstanding which exists between artist and craftsman.

The enterprising endeavour of the process-block maker is to perfect his process to produce a clean, bright, faultless piece of technical work; a process which shall produce from all kinds of originals an equally brilliant print, so that, when he is called to reproduce a special effect which the artist may desire, he seems incapable of understanding as desirable anything which falls short of his own arbitrary standard. It is as though the artist's colourman said to the painter, you must varnish all your picture so as to show the full richness and gloss of the colours, no matter whether the painter reckoned on some degree of dulness to give a certain effect.

LINE BLOCK LIGHTENED BY ROULETTE.

(Original 7 x 6.)

So the material maker will aim at supplying canvas or board of as fine and smooth a surface as possible, and it is at first difficult to persuade him that the artist is right in desiring a coarse, rough surface. The process man and material maker are ever on the side of polish, brilliancy, and fineness.

Execution and craft invariably seem to be at war with feeling and art, and I would strongly caution my reader against being too much concerned about the relative virtues of various processes, or too much prejudiced by what others may have to say. Whatever your artist friend may advise is pretty certain to be discounted by your block-maker; and in course of time, and after experience, you will probably form your own individual opinion, which will be at variance with both.

It is at this stage that more particular mention may be made of the use of the *roulette* to correct by hand, on the zinc block, the misinterpretations of the process. The roulette consists of a sharp-edged toothed wheel of minute proportions, which is passed backwards and forwards across lines which have come up too black, thus breaking such lines into tiny dots, which therefore print greyer.

It is well to know that such a revision of the block, as first turned out, is possible, and we shall sometimes be glad to make use of it. Still, as before pointed out, such hand-work must not be relied upon.

CHAPTER XI.

OTHER METHODS ADAPTED FOR LINE REPRODUCTION.

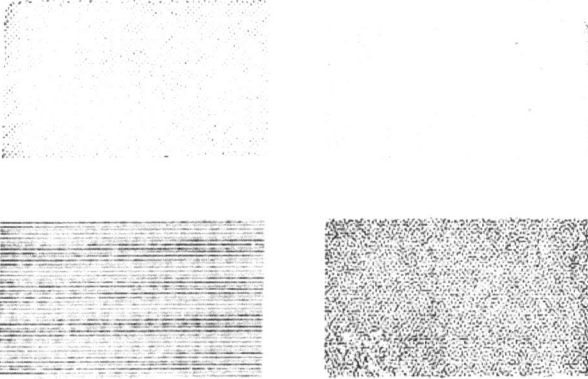

W hen a large space is required to be covered with an even tint, an immense saving of labour and time may be effected by the use of "Shading media"; but beyond a mere saving of labour they may, if discreetly used, be made to produce some very desirable effects.

If applied to the entire surface, the result is very like a half-tone process block in appearance. This is seen in the illustration on page 85, in which the shading medium has been applied everywhere except in the few white spots.

Such an application is particularly useful for evening or twilight subjects, but it is more usual to employ them locally, especially for skies. They are also largely used by some artists for figures, in the manner shown in illustration on page 65, in which the shading is so effectively used on the waistcoat and hat of the man.

The pattern of the tint varies greatly, there being more than a dozen distinct designs, a few examples of which are given on page 91.

These shading media are introduced on to the zinc block after printing from the negative (see Chap. VII.), for which purpose transparent sheets of gelatine, on which the required pattern has been engraved and previously inked, are used. By pressing these on to the albumen or other surface of the block, an ink impression is transferred, which accordingly protects the surface during etching in the same manner as the rest of the picture. The "shading" need not be restricted to the blank spaces only, but may be pressed on to any part or the whole of the block; and there is no reason why two or more different patterns should not be used in combination on the same subject. The gelatine sheets being transparent, the process worker can see exactly where to apply them, and can do so with considerably intricacy.

SHADING MEDIUM ON PEN SKETCH VIGNETTE.

(*Original 5 x 4.*)

In sending to the etchers a drawing in which a shading medium is to be introduced, the practice is to mark such portions as are to be shaded by scribbling over with blue pencil; this is at once understood better than written instructions. It had better be stated whether a dark or light tint be required; also whether it is to be vignetted or shaded all over. Vignetting is the most usual, as seen in the accompanying block, page 92. It is usual for the process people to make a slight additional charge for the introduction of tints; especially if at all complicated. And, of course, if special experiments in the combination of various tints be intended, requiring special care, fair consideration must be made for the additional trouble and labour.

Like most mechanical aids to drawing, shading media must be adopted with discretion, and they can at best be considered as a poor substitute for pure hand-work; they economise time and are useful in an emergency, but I should certainly caution the beginner against the too frequent use of them.

An ingenious method of imparting a certain greyness to some portions of a drawing is illustrated by the accompanying sketch "Near Berry Head."

This is known as "Splatter work," and consists of sprinkling minute dots of the black drawing fluid wherever required.

The drawing is first executed in the usual way, and all portions which are not to be "splattered" upon are covered over with pieces of paper cut to the necessary shape and size.

A stiff bristle brush is then inked; nothing serving for the purpose better than an ordinary tooth-brush. Holding the brush in the left hand, with the bristles downwards, the bristles are to be briskly stroked with any handy stick of wood; in this manner a spray of tiny dots of ink is splashed on to the paper beneath.

NEAR BERRY HEAD.

Pen drawing—foreground dotted by "splatter" work. (Original 6¼ x 5.)

Perhaps a finer and more regular spray may be obtained by taking the brush in the right hand and brushing it over the fine teeth of a comb, by which means the splashes can be with more certainty directed to a particular spot. Superfluous ink should be struck off the brush before sprinkling the drawing, and some portions of the protecting paper masks can be removed before others if some of the "splattering" be required to extend further.

It will be best to use an indelible or fixed ink for this work, as, even after practice, some ugly splashes are apt to occur, which will have to be afterwards corrected with Chinese white. Splatter work is more largely practised in America, and is just one of those tricks which in dexterous hands is sometimes so peculiarly happy in its results, and yet so apparently unresponsive in others.

We now come to consider an important group of drawing methods, known as "Scratch boards."

In speaking of white cardboards, reference was made to clay surface boards, and the possibility of removing any fault by scraping with a knife. We have now to do with a selection of boards in which the clay surface and the scraping-out possibilities are carried to the utmost practical extent, and made use of as a chief method of representation, not as a means to correct mistakes. These boards are of two principal kinds: 1st. White, on which are impressed white indented lines, giving the whole a ribbed appearance; and, 2nd, Black reticulations, or lines printed at right angles to the impressed grain or ribs.

Canvas-like reticulations, irregular grain or "Aquatint" dots, and diagonal or vertical lines, are the most useful patterns (of which there are many); they may be obtained at F.W. Devoe & C.T. Raynolds Co. and most of the dealers in materials, and are known as scratch-out, scrape-out or stipple boards.

Both boards are of a somewhat similar description, differing only in the method of producing the pattern. In the white boards the marks are *impressed*; whereas in the black ones they are *printed*.

Taking the black patterns first, the grain printed thereon supplies us with a flat grey tint composed of numerous fine black lines; this for convenience we will call the *full* tint. Now if we gently scrape the clay surface with the sharp point of a knife, moving it *across* the black lines, they will be removed from the top of the impressed ridges which cross at right angles, thus at once converting the *black lines* into rows of *black dots*, and giving a lighter tint which we will call a half-tint. Closely examine the accompanying series of specimens, and this will be at once recognised.

THE SCRAPER.

No. I.
DOTS.

No. II.
HORIZONTAL LINES.

No. III.
DIAGONAL LINES.

No. IV.
AQUATINT.

EXAMPLES OF BLACK GRAIN "SCRAPE BOARDS." (*Original size.*)

In No. 1 we have a board with parallel ruling, as supplied by the makers; in No. 2, a few strokes of the knife have converted some of the lines into dots; in No. 3, the knife has been used more vigorously, scraping away lines altogether and thus producing plain whites. This, then, gives us full tint, half-tint, and white. Now if we work with pencil or pen on the full tint, building up the drawing precisely as if drawing on plain white card, and then scrape out, as just illustrated, it will be seen what a wide range of "tones" will be suggested.

No. I.   No. II.   No. III.

The drawing is to be put in first either with crayon, pencil, or ink, and the scraping done afterwards; by this means any mistakes can readily be scratched out; no small consolation to the unpractised. But, on the other hand, a faulty scratch or scrape cannot be rectified, hence the greater need for care.

The manner of handling the knife (an ordinary penknife, or a specially constructed blade, may be used) differs a good deal in individual workers, but the safer manner is perhaps to keep the knife well up and nearly vertical. Avoid outlines, allowing the different degrees of tint to separate one object from another, as one would do in a wash drawing, and proceed somewhat in the manner illustrated by the accompanying figures.

A MISTY MOONRISE.

(*Original 4 x 2½.*)

(Original 4 x 2½.)

One of the difficulties to be guarded against is the too great evidence of scraping, the knife marks often revealing themselves much more plainly in the reproduction than in the original, also the too sudden contrast between the full tint and the scratched half-tint. Notice in the two accompanying sketches on diagonal grain boards, by Mr. C.J. Vine, how the full tint, when it meets the half-tint, is broken up by slight irregular scratches; especially is this seen in the sky of "A Misty Moonrise." In this sketch, sky, sea, and the sails of the two more distant boats, are almost entirely made up by the diagonal tint and the scraped half-tint. Only in the hulls of the boats and the sails of the nearest boat is pen-work introduced, the lines being drawn diagonally from right to left, at right angles to the grain of the full tint.[6]

PEN AND INK ON BLACK LINE SCRAPE BOARD. FIRST STAGE.

(Original 5¾ x 3.)

PEN AND INK ON BLACK LINE SCRAPE BOARD WITH WHITE SCRAPED OUT.

(Original 5½ x 3¼.)

A more rapid way of obtaining an effect can hardly be imagined than by these "scraped" boards, and in good hands, or with practice, the effects obtainable are often very charming. The drawings should, as a rule, be not greatly larger than the reproduction intended—a reduction of one-third or one-half being about the best. All the different kinds of black grain boards are treated in the same manner as above described.

PENCIL ON VERTICAL GRAIN WHITE SCRAPE BOARD.

By C.J. Vine. (Original 4 x 3.)

Now the use of white grained boards is less a scraping method than pure line drawing, much of the "line" being almost mechanically produced by drawing upon the "ribbed" surface with pencil. We know if we place a piece of paper upon a rough, cloth-covered book and rub a blacklead pencil over it we get a mottled effect, the blacks and whites of which are reproductions of the projections and depressions on the book cover; so if we draw on a ribbed surface clay-board with pen and ink, the ink follows elevation and depression in one continuous pen stroke. If, however, we draw with a black pencil, without undue pressure, the pencil passes from one elevation to another, or from one "rib" to another, and thus forms a broken or dotted line, which, although in actual colour as black as an ink line, yet being broken and not solid, will reproduce lighter or greyer. A number of adjacent pencil lines would therefore produce a flat tint of dots, very similar to the tint of a "half-tone" block or a "shading medium," in addition to which, and upon which, ink lines may be made to produce deeper blacks. On the accompanying illustration are pencil marks and ink strokes drawn on a piece of grained white board, the grain or "ribs" being vertical. To the left, a single detached pencil stroke forming dotted lines; next are adjacent pencil lines constituting a grained tint, something very like the full tone of the black-grained blocks before considered, and coarser or finer in proportion as the pencil is pressed more or less heavily; next we have some pen and ink lines, the difference of which will at once be seen; and finally, a mixture of pencil and pen, on which the knife has subsequently been used to scratch some small lights. This exhausts the practical possibilities of white grained scrape boards.

No 1

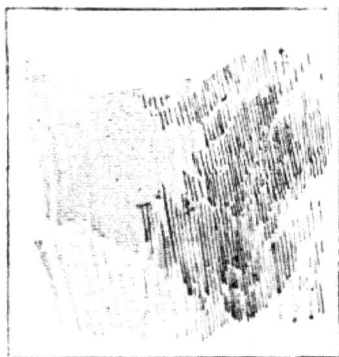

N. II

No III

The accompanying sketches will show somewhat the kind of things obtainable.

PENCIL AND PEN ON VERTICAL LINE WHITE SCRAPE BOARD.

By C.J. Vine. (Original 4 x 3.)

Reduction causes a very marked improvement, and the drawings should be looked at from time to time whilst in progress with a "diminishing" glass. An indelible ink should be used, or one that does not penetrate but rests on the surface: such as ivory-black, lamp-black, or Indian ink. Instead of pencil, a stick of lithographic chalk will be of advantage. In the first place, the greyness of pencil is deceptive, and reproduces blacker than we expect, moreover pencil rubs and smears; not so lithographic chalk, which does not rub, and is black. The scratching or scraping must be the final stage of a drawing, as only solid pen marks can be put on the white board after the grained clay surface has been removed.

DRAWINGS IN PENCIL OR CHALK ON ROUGH PAPERS.

By the foregoing description of pencil or chalk drawing on ribbed surfaces, we see how a pencil drawing may be translated by an ordinary line zinco block, instead of the more expensive half-tone process described in the earlier chapters. The pencil or crayon point, in passing over a rough or broken surface, forms a series of dots instead of a continuous line. The same thing occurs when pencil is used on a rough surface drawing paper. Such pencillings, being examined, are found to be lead marks, interspersed with minute interstices of white paper, the whole giving a sort of grey tint of greater or less intensity.

For broad sketchy effects such a drawing method is exceedingly valuable; some very delightful things may be done without the least appearance of the mechanical.

SEWARDSTONE MARSHES.

Drawing on Conté crayon on rough paper. (Original 6 x 4.)

As may be readily understood from the accompanying examples, such drawings are best adapted for purely artistic impressions, and not for the portrayal of detail.

Practically any paper may be used which is white, and whose surface is sufficiently rough; some particular kinds, about to be mentioned, have proved especially successful under experiment. Any material may be used to draw with, preference being given to a black substance which will not smear or rub on being touched.

A good "B" blacklead pencil has the advantage of being pleasant to handle, and capable of being used with a sufficiently fine point to render some details; it has, however, the decided disadvantage of "rubbing" with a very little touching, and the strokes, although fairly intense, are not so black as crayon;

hence, in reproduction, many portions which were expected to come out soft and delicate, reproduce much too black. We have, then, for our selection, Hardmuth's or Conté's crayons, made in several degrees, and also made into cedar-wood pencils—a cleaner and more handy form. Neither of these is, unfortunately, free from the disadvantage of blurring when rubbed, and will hence require to be fixed before being sent away; the photo-engraver, in the press of his business, rarely failing to subject drawings to a severe test.

Fixing may be best effected by treating the drawing with a solution of one part pure gum mastic dissolved in seven parts methylated spirit.

In Lemercier's lithographic crayons we have a drawing medium which gives as satisfactory results as the Conté or Hardmuth, and does not blur; it therefore saves the trouble of fixing. Being greasy, they should be used in a porte-crayon. They are made in three degrees as to hardness, the No. 1 being the hardest and best suited for drawing the limited amount of detail which is possible with crayons.

So long as the drawing is not too heavily worked upon, a surprising improvement is secured by reducing. A reduction of one-half is not too much.

As to the papers to be used, the following may be mentioned as only some which I have tested, and which others have spoken well of, but there must be a great many other rough surface materials well worth a trial.

Of the well-known Whatman papers, both the "Hot-pressed" and "Not," the latter being, perhaps, preferable.

A French paper, Allongé, has a very pleasing surface grain, and may be used on the right or wrong side with different results; the right side being the rougher, and perhaps the better.

CRAYON DRAWING ON ALLONGÉ PAPER.

Small whites in Chinese white. (Original 9 x 6.)

Next, we have Lalanne and Michallet or Ingres papers, and some examples of crayon drawing on these are here given.

CRAYON ON PYRAMID PAPER NO. 2.

Small whites in Chinese white. (Original 7 x 6.)

The most noticeable feature in these will be the lines, or grain, formed by the texture of the paper; this grain is apparently more perceptible when vertical, but if the paper is turned round so that the lines come into a horizontal position, they are much less discernible in the finished sketch.

In many respects the effect of these papers is a good deal similar to that gained by using the white lined clay-boards; the grain being, however, less mechanical. In like manner the crayon sketch may be effectively helped by the addition of pen and ink, or fine brush work. Scraping out, however, is not within its capabilities; though Chinese white, if applied fairly solidly, may successfully stop-out small lights or efface errors.

CRAYON ON PYRAMID NO. 1.

(Original 9 x 6.)

Other papers which may be attempted are Arnold's drawing papers, rough surface cartridge, various crayon papers, &c. Such houses as Penrose & Co., Amwell Street, E.C., London, or F.W. Devoe & C.T. Raynolds Co., of New York, would probably supply patterns and information in this respect.

A paper known as Pyramid Grained paper has a granulated surface, breaking the crayon marks into a succession of dots rather than broken lines, and often yields very pleasing results; it is made in two varying degrees, No. 1 having a grain of 15,000 "pyramids" to the square inch, and No. 2, 9,000.

For a further variation in effect, a drawing may be executed in crayon or pencil on a fairly smooth paper previously pressed into close contact with any rough surface, such as sandpaper or canvas. The unsized side of a canvas for oil painting, or the cover of a book, will answer the purpose; openness of work, and the amount of ultimate reduction desirable, being depended upon and controlled accordingly.

The following sketches, by Mr. C.J. Vine, on Michallet and Lallane papers (pp. 111, 113, 115, 117), are pure untouched crayon work, reproduced by zinc line etching, so that these drawings may be safely entrusted to this cheapest and least sympathetic process; though there can be little doubt that the swelled gelatine would render fuller justice to work of this class.

CHAPTER XII.

MECHANICALAIDS TO DRAUGHTSMANSHIP—DRAWING AND SKETCHING FROM NATURE.

The various methods whereby illustrations may be made for reproduction have now been reviewed, if not exhaustively, at least with sufficient completeness to enable the reader to start making those actual experiments in practice without which the most exact description is useless.

But thus far, with the exception of such cases in which it is possible to use a photogram and reproduce it by "half-tone" process, some ability to draw, some certain amount of native artistry on the part of the student, has been taken for granted.

Now, while in wash drawings, crayon, or pencil sketches, "scrape" boards, and the like, there must be some amount of instinctive artistic ability, not only to guide the hand in execution but to govern taste, idea, and selection; yet in simple line drawing with the pen, without any art knowledge or technical ability, it may be possible to produce a perfectly reproducible drawing, fulfilling in every way the essential duty of an illustration. And if this be so, there is no reason why very many more writers should not illustrate what they have to say, making matters more intelligible and producing a more lasting impression.

For the purpose we shall require a photogram to commence with, and here is a use and an application of photography not always fully realised or appreciated. A man may be possessed of considerable taste and judgment in the selecting of a view, or particular aspect of a building, and yet be utterly lacking in ability to put down on paper correctly what he sees; that is, he is not a good draughtsman. No particular taste in selecting a position may be needed, or possessed, and yet it may be desirable to portray an object, or scene, and it is to such men that the camera becomes so important as an indirect means to illustration. Indirect because, as already pointed out, the reproduction of a photogram by half-tone process (the only way of reproducing a photogram for type machine printing) is attended with difficulties, and cannot always be resorted to. The half-tone block is not suitable for the most rapid printing in newspapers, &c.; its results are not all that could be wished; it is more expensive and takes longer to make, apart from such other drawbacks pointed out in an earlier chapter. Therefore it is desirable to see how we can utilise a photogram so as to produce the simpler, and often more acceptable, line block from it, and do this by a more mechanical method than re-drawing, or copying from it.

Probably the first easy method that will suggest itself will be to make a tracing from it on tracing paper, and then with carbon paper transfer it to the desired card, &c.

There is no objection to such a course, except that it is not always attended with equal satisfaction. To begin with, a photogram is often so dark in parts as to prevent our seeing many details through the tracing paper; also, however careful, if we are tracing a face, the slight deviation in tracing over the outlines and features, which is almost unavoidable, and further variations when afterwards transferring, will often seriously interfere with the likeness —presuming a likeness to be required.

STUDY OF TREES.

Crayon drawing on Lalanne paper; vertical grain. (Original 8 x 4½.)

An avoidance of error and saving of time may be effected by making a fairly pale print and, having "fixed" it, cover the back with the scribble of a blue pencil or chalk.

We can now place this down upon the card board or paper to be drawn upon, and carefully go over everything that is to be drawn with a sharp hard point, which will leave a blue outline sketch which can then be inked in, and the blue need not be rubbed out afterwards as it will not appear in reproduction.

In the same way the original photogram can be used with a piece of *blue* carbon paper instead of chalking the back of the print. No attempt should be made to draw in all the details of a photogram, but only such salient points as may be required for illustration.

Another method is as follows:—Make the photogram in the ordinary way, but on "plain salted paper," or "Matt silver sensitised paper," which has been previously prepared by immersion for a short while in a solution of ammonium chlorate, 100 grains; gelatine, 10 grains; water, 10 ounces.

The photogram is to be fixed and washed, toning being unnecessary; when dry it can be drawn upon with a "*fixed*" or *indelible* black ink, carefully putting in just what parts are needed and disregarding the rest of the picture. As soon as the ink is dry, the print is immersed in a bath of mercury bichlorate and alcohol, when the photogram will gradually disappear, leaving the black ink lines on plain white paper. Nothing more is required beyond mounting on card to fit it for reproduction. Of course corrections can be made and stains, &c., be removed with Chinese white. Should it be desired to restore the bleached photogram, it can be done by immersing in a weak solution of soda hyposulphite.

The foregoing method is one given by Mr. C.G. Harper in his book "Drawing for Reproduction"; it appears, however, needlessly elaborate, and I presume mercury *bichloride* is intended and not bichlorate. Even with care the photographic image is sometimes slow to get rid of, and will often refuse altogether to leave the clear white blank we require.

ADVANCING TWILIGHT.

Crayon drawing on Lalanne paper; horizontal grain. (Original 10½ x 6.)

A photographic print, however, on either albumenised or "Matt" paper will certainly disappear utterly if subjected to the following bath, for which formula I am indebted to Mr. E.J. Wall:—

Iodine	1	grain
Iodide of Potassium	10	grains
Cyanide of Potassium	20	"
Water	102	"

This is a similar solution as is used to remove ink-stains from linen, &c.

The print may also be bleached by sponging over with the following preparation, recommended by W. Ethelbert Henry:—

Saturated Solution Iodine in Alcohol	1 part
" " Cyanide of Potassium in Water	2 parts
Water	2 "

After which the print is to be washed well for a few minutes.

Of course the reason for using a "fixed" ink in such processes is obvious.

Yet another method on similar lines, but even simpler in operation. A certain photographic printing paper called "Ferro-prussiate" paper gives, on exposure to light, a *blue* image, and only requires washing in water to "fix" or make it permanent. This blue print can now be used for drawing upon, as in the previous instance, only that the photographic image, being blue, does not need to be bleached, and will not interfere with the reproduction of the black lines drawn upon it.

If for any reason it be desired to get rid of the blue print, this can be bleached by immersion in water containing a little common washing soda.

BEACHY HEAD.

Crayon drawing on Michallet paper, right side. (Original 8½ x 5½.)

Thus from a photogram of even the most elaborate subject an absolutely correct drawing may be made fit for reproduction without the illustrator having any knowledge or skill as a draughtsman.

By placing the unskilled in such a position, photography appears to have removed the last obstacle to the more frequent use of appropriate illustration; and the ease with which both pleasing and *accurate* outlines can be made should render inexcusable the shamefully untruthful "sketches" which every day appear in newspaper and magazine.

The method of drawing on thin transfer paper with transfer ink, and then placing the drawing direct on to a zinc block, hardly needs to be referred to here. Such a simple means of placing the image on the zinc and then etching is necessarily of limited application, neither reduction nor enlargement is possible, and photography is not employed; it is merely a mechanical etching of the zinc in all parts not protected by the ink image, as transferred from the drawing in transfer ink, and is used for very rapid and imperfect portraits,

&c., in the commoner class of newspaper work.

And now, whatever be the special characteristics and advantages of the camera, it is by no means my intention to advocate its use where even only a moderate amount of native artistic ability exists; and, in all probability, the possessor of such ability will more frequently prefer to use his sketch-book than his camera—and this is as it should be. There is always something of freshness about a first original sketch, be it in whatsoever medium, a quality which the most careful copy fails to repeat.

This brings us to consider whether it would not be well to make our first impressions or sketches in such a manner that they could be handed to the process worker right away; and we shall then have to consider what medium and what materials are suitable for "drawing from life." Certainly the ordinary pencil sketch, as taken from the pocket sketch-book, would not do. In the first place such sketches would rarely be vigorous enough, and whatever vigour they possessed would be sadly diminished by rubbing and the pressure of the opposite page.

A SUSSEX LANE.

Crayon drawing on Michallet paper, wrong side of paper used. (Original 9 x 4½.)

Very few have successfully drawn from life in pen and ink. Some few well-known caricaturists and figure draughtsmen do so, and attain success purely through their splendid dash and spirit, but such things are forbidden the average man with whom the pen drawing is a matter of delicate care. But there seems no reason why the lithographic crayon on rough paper should not be thus utilised, and slight "touchings-up" added afterwards. In this way we might often have ready for immediate reproduction a sketch containing some of that spontaneous feeling which is so noticeable when glancing through the pages of an artist's sketch-book.

I have noticed in some a very false idea existing with regard to draughting in a picture with pencil before using the pen and ink. Now I do not hesitate to say that the careful sketching in of the subject in pencil is essential to all except the genius, and I am not writing for the genius, who knows more than I can tell him and can dispense with what he does not know. There is nothing to be ashamed of in drawing first in pencil; one might perhaps be able to draw in quite as correctly with the pen, but the advantage of a pencil outline as a guide is that it gives more time and leisure thought for carefully considering the pen work before putting it in. By this course there is less danger of confused hesitating lines. From the first let the ink lines be clear, distinct, and black; no "messing about," to quote Mr. Blackburn's expressive phrase; be decided as to the sort of shading you are going to put in a certain place and put it there, once for all, and don't touch it again. Avoid, by constant self-restraint, over-elaboration or too much laboured detail; let each part of the drawing be *finished* from the first, and do not return to it and work on it over and over again. And the first step to ensuring this precision will be by carefully pencilling everything, *indicating* only where shading is to come. When the pen and ink drawing is completed, carefully erase the pencil marks with *bread crumbs*; do not use indiarubber, which will be sure to abrade the surface, and probably break the continuity of the ink lines.

As we become more conversant with the possibilities of the zinco process, an intimacy which can only be brought by an experience built up of experiments and failures, we shall find it possible to sometimes leave in certain of the pencilling (allowing, of course, for their coming up as black as ink), but for the beginner such a practice is not recommended, as it is nearly sure to end in disappointment.

There are many interesting modifications of recognised means which are possible to the experienced—especially the production of what may be termed "mixed drawings," either for reproduction in half-tone or line, drawings in which in order to produce less ordinary effects, wash, pen, and pencil are employed combinedly; but, by the time my gentle reader has reached a stage when he may advisedly attempt such excursions from the orthodox path, he will have passed beyond the sphere of this book and will be entitled to that liberty which art permits to its practitioners.

In the meantime let me ask the student to repress for a time his more lofty aspirations, and content himself with patiently learning to produce—not a charming sketch, a delightful drawing, but—a drawing in which there is as much of artistic or pictorial merit as is compatible with the requirements of the process of reproduction. If you are drawing professedly for reproduction, no blame can attach to you if you "bear in mind during the production of your drawing the necessity of its making a good block, with as little sacrifice of artistic quality as may be."

An exalted position as an art is not necessarily claimed for drawing or painting for reproduction; but how much of that difficult-to-be-defined quality which we call "artistic" exists in it, depends not so much upon the method, the means, or the application, as it does on those who work at it and their motive. Apart from this, viewed from the lowest aspect, its utility is beyond question, and at the present time it is an application of fine art showing the most vitality of any.

The books devoted to the subject which have already been written, have perhaps given too much attention to the actual processes of reproduction—they have not appealed to the illustrator; or else, while professing to be books of instruction in practice, have dealt rather with the theory of illustration and the comparison of styles. It seemed to me there was need for a simple description of methods for the enlightening of a beginner: an elementary guide; a first step; in short, a Handbook of illustration.